DIRTY WORDS: psychoanalytic insights

ARIEL C. ARANGO, M.D.

JASON ARONSON
Northvale, New Jersey
London

10 9 8 7 6 5 4 3 2 1

Library of Congress Cataloging-in-Publication Data

Arango, Ariel C.
Dirty words : psychoanalytic insights / Ariel C. Arango.
p. cm.
Bibliography: p.
Includes index.
ISBN 0-87668-855-5
1. Words, Obscene. 2. Psychoanalytic interpretation. I. Title.
[DNLM: 1. Language. 2. Psychoanalytic Interpretation. WM 460.7
A662d]
P410.027A73 1989
401'.9–dc20
DNLM/DLC
for Library of Congress 89-6745
CIP

Manufactured in the United States of America.Jason Aronson Inc. offers books and cassettes. For information and catalog write to Jason Aronson Inc., 230 Livingston Street, Northvale, New Jersey 07647.

To the Spanish psychoanalyst, Dr. Angel Garma, with whom I have gone through a natural, advantageous, plain as well as deep psychoanalysis

Contents

If we did not have freedom of action, in the field of morals as well as in the field of politics and social problems, our freedom of expression would be limited to the propaganda to support the current state of things, and to prevent all innovation.

William O. Douglas
Judge of the Supreme Court
of the United States of America
(The People's Rights I. C., 1957)

1

DIRTY WORDS

"Because no matter what is done or said, our similarities with the savage are still more numerous than our differences . . ."

SIR JAMES FRAZER
(*The Golden Bough*,
Chapter XXIII, 1922)

I

It surprises us to learn that there are some societies—"primitive" societies, we call them—in which the mere utterance of certain words is strictly forbidden. And yet, the fact is that in all primitive societies one finds such taboos. From Siberia to meridional India, from the Mongols of Tartaria to the Tuaregs of the Sahara, from Japan to Oriental Africa, and in the Philippines, in the Nicobar Islands of Borneo, in Madagascar and Tasmania and in several Indian tribes of continental America, one finds that particular words cannot be said. It may be a personal name, or a specific relative's name (especially the most intimate blood-related persons) or the names of the dead, or of a god or other sacred being. The individual who inadvertently or deliberately lets such a name slip from his lips is liable to severe punishment. The sanctions have included imprisonment among some tribes in Thailand to the death penalty among the Guajiros in Colombia. In ancient Tahiti, the way to the scaffold was taken not only by the daring person who had pronounced the forbidden word but by his whole family as well. Even in ancient Greece and Rome, it appears that the mere utterance of certain words was taboo.

The word *taboo*, itself, is of Polynesian origin, and interestingly, has two opposite meanings: on the one hand, sacred or consecrated; and on the other, impure, prohibited, dangerous, and disturbing. It is anything that regularly awakens a "sacred fear"[1] in us. The anthropologist, Sir James George Frazer (1854–1941) states in *The Golden Bough* (1922) that,

> Unable to differentiate between words and objects, the savage generally imagines that the link between a name and the nominated object or subject is not a mere arbitrary and ideologic association but a true and substantial bond. . . .[2]

This materialistic conception of the nature of words that primitives have, undoubtedly arouses within us an indefinite but strong sensation of superiority. We know that words are only the names of things. We accept the banning of certain actions, but not a ban on naming them. It would be as if during Prohibition in the United States, not only the sale of whisky had been forbidden but the reading of the bottle labels in a loud voice as well. This curious peculiarity of the primitive mind awakens not only astonishment but also a fatherly understanding in us, because being civilized men, we can definitely differentiate reality from words. Or can't we?

II

> Vi baccio mille volte. La mia anima baccia la vostra, mio cazzo, mio cuore sono innamorati di voi. Baccio el vostro gentil culo e tutta la vostra persona.[3]

This quotation is taken from a love letter (*Lettres d'amour de Voltaire à sa niece, Paris,* 1957) written in Italian by Voltaire, the French philosopher (1694–1778), in December 1745. Translated into English it means:

> I kiss you a thousand times. My soul kisses yours, my cock, my heart are in love with you. I kiss your nice ass and all your person.

We are undoubtedly surprised by the letter. We are not accustomed to the open expression of obscene feelings, at least not among respectable people. We have learned that eroticism may be hinted at, but never openly declared. That is why the word *cock* strikes us even more strongly than the disturbing word *ass.* We are not used to reading it in serious writing and we feel a sensation of embarrassment, discomfort, rejection, shame, and yes, maybe even pleasure too.

There are other accepted, or at least more tolerated words to describe the sensuous parts of the body. Let us substitute, then, *penis* for *cock,* and *rear end* for *ass.* The modified passage reads as follows:

> I kiss you a thousand times. My soul kisses yours, my penis, my heart are in love with you. I kiss your nice rear end and all your person.

We have modified only two words but the atmosphere of the former letter has vanished. It has lost strength, intensity, and voluptuousness. It neither disturbs nor discomforts us in the same way. This is obviously a curious transformation. The words *penis* and *cock,* like the words *rear end* and *ass,* are synonyms; they refer to the same parts of our anatomy. Yet our emotional evaluation of the different terms is not the same. Furthermore, cock and ass are forbidden words. They cannot be used in formal conversation, nor can they be employed by newspapers, radio, or television. One would not expect to hear them from a school teacher or a professor at a university. This, of course, increases our curiosity. If they refer to the same aspect of reality, why are some terms forbidden while others are not? Even taking into account the universality of some sexual restrictiveness in all societies, it is still worth asking why the words *penis* and *rear end* are less censored than *cock* and *ass.*

In any case, these brief considerations bring us to an interesting discovery regarding our own sophisticated, contemporary culture: namely, forbidden words exist here, too. Certain aspects of reality may be named with some terms but not with others. We need not make a long voyage to an unknown country to find such prohibitions. It has been rightly said that the last thing an inhabitant of the sea would discover would be the water itself. In short, taboo words exist among us too, and for a long time we have revealingly qualified them. We call them *dirty words.*

2

HALLUCINATIONS

"Dreams are hallucinatory experiences, and these, as I have already pointed out, could also be called in more colloquial terms experiences of fright or of panic of the sleeper."

ANGEL GARMA

(New Contributions to the Psychoanalysis of the Dream, IV, 1970)

I

What is the origin of this peculiar taboo?

Basically, we notice that dirty words always refer to parts of the body, secretions, or behavior patterns that arouse sexual desire. "Dirty" words are always obscene words. But, what is obscene? Let us try to find the historical origin of the word. Its etymology is obscure. It is possibly a corruption or modification of the Latin word *scena* that literally means "out of scene."[1] Obscene would then be that which should be off scene, that is, off the theater of life. Shakespeare (1564–1616), in *As You Like It*, II, 7, magnificently expressed this similarity between life and theatre:

> "All the world's a stage,
> And all the men and women merely players."[2]

The "dirty" word or the obscene word is the one that breaks the rules of the social scene; the one that dares express what should not be seen or heard. That is why obscenity and pornography are words that often go hand in hand. They are related words. Pornography comes from the Greek *pornographes*, which literally means "writing on harlots," that is, the description of the life of prostitutes.[3] Obscenity, or "off scene" sexuality, is precisely the métier of these women. Obscenity is thus the genus and pornography one of its species. This knowledge is undoubtedly fruitful for our research. We know now that dirty words are "dirty" because they are obscene, and they are obscene because they name without hypocrisy, euphemism, or modesty what should never be mentioned in public: the true and lewd sexuality. Furthermore, these words often carry a hallucinatory force. They arouse the picture of the sexual organ or scene in a most vivid way, and they also arouse strong licentious feelings. This peculiarity is shown to be of great importance in psychoanalysis, inasmuch as the therapeutic process of psychoanalysis is based, almost miraculously, on words; or, as Hamlet disdainfully said, "Words, words, words."

Yet for psychoanalysis, if not for Hamlet, there are no vain words. On the contrary, words, all of them, are always revealing. It is through them that unconscious conflicts become conscious. That is the secret of the method and of the cure. Sigmund Freud (1856–1939) stated this at length in *The Psychoanalytic Method* (1904):

> The task the psychoanalytic method tends to carry out may be expressed in many ways, all of them basically alike. It might be said that the goal of the therapy is to suppress amnesia. Once all the gaps have been bridged and all mysterious affections of psychic life have been clarified it is impossible for the disease to last or even to recur. It may also be claimed that the aim striven for is to shatter all repressions since the resulting psychic state is the same as that attained once amnesia has been overcome. Applying a wider formulation, it may also be stated that the objective involves trying to make conscious that which is unconscious; this is achieved by deflating resistance.[4]

The patient, while on the couch, tells the psychoanalyst all the ideas that come to his mind in the exact order they appear. This is the widely known method of "free association." It is the psychoanalyst who interprets the hidden link behind this multifarious stream of ideas and feelings. Needless to say, any censorship is banished. Free associations are beyond good, evil, logic, pain, disgust, anguish, or shame. Every word is welcome, and that includes, of course, "dirty" words.

Actually it is impossible to overrate the therapeutic value of these condemned words. No treatment can be thought to be over *rebus bene gesta* (having everything gone well) if the patient does not allow himself to utter obscene words. Failing to do this, no success is possible. A patient who relates his sexual life in the terminology characteristic of an anatomy or physiology book is not revealing his story but rather is delivering a summary, as scientific, cold, and impersonal as a medical book. Moral conscience is to be blamed; it did not allow him to narrate in a warm, even hot, fashion his love life. It is the psychoanalyst's task to point this out without hesitation or mercy. For, quite often, the patient himself ignores this. He deludes himself. He naively imagines that simply speaking about sexuality is the same as living it (many psychoanalysts also have this delusion). However, it is clear that there is a great difference between *telling* and *confiding* an intimacy.

Freud's own attitude on the subject was ambiguous and unquestionably mistaken. In revealing to the world the psychoanalysis of an 18-year-old girl–the famous case of Dora–in *Fragment of an Analysis of a Case of Hysteria* (1905), Freud maintained:

> . . . sexual relationships are discussed with total freedom, the true name of the sexual functions and organs is used, and the chaste reader will therefore extract from his reading the certainty that I have not been intimidated to speak of such subjects and in such terminology with a young woman.[5]

Whoever reads this captivating presentation will notice that Freud's statement is not reliable. Were sexual functions and organs given their true names? Definitely not. The father of psychoanalysis did not use obscene words but scientific terms, quite often even Latin words. Thus he referred to sucking the penis or licking the vulva as *coito per os*. What ensued, then, was an erotic conversation between an adolescent and an adult; but it was an expurgated conversation. "In my consultations," he later stated, "I give both sexual acts and organs their technical names."[6]

Such a way of talking does not, however, arouse true feelings but only their muffled version. They are musical notes played in mute tones whereas psychoanalysis seeks the most heartfelt melodies. In the long run its purpose is nothing but *à la recherche des sentiments perdus,* the search of lost affections.

In this as in all his work Freud always made use of chaste dialect. He suffered from what he himself called "the hereditary vice of virtue."[7] He was a discreet man, and discretion is a trait incompatible with the true account of human passions. In fact, even though he shocked the world by revealing the sexual desire of every child for his parents, Freud, himself, was a chaste man. When he was young he thoroughly participated in the prudery of his time. He did not allow his 26-year-old fiancée, Martha Bernays (1861–1951), to read Henry Fielding's (1707–1754) *Tom Jones* (1749)–considered by many to be the best English novel–because he thought it inappropriate for her honest soul.[8] On another occasion, he felt he had to apologize to her for merely having mentioned in a letter the feet of the Venus de Milo. At another time, when Martha told him she wanted to stay in the house of an old friend who, as she delicately put it, "had got married before the wedding," Freud absolutely forbade her any contact with such a source of moral contamination.[9]

His was not only a youthful zeal. In 1920, when he was 64 years old, he was taken aback when Georg Groddeck (1866–1934), a German psychoanalyst, joined the International Psychoanalytic Congress in The Hague – escorted by his lover![10] It was a typical reaction in those Victorian times. This period took its name from Queen Victoria of England (1819–1901), but such prudery was common throughout 19th century Europe. The period was characterized by strict prohibitions involving "not only true proper sexual words, images and things, but also whatever might be associated, symbolically, to sexuality."[11] The founder of psychoanalysis was, no doubt, a child of his time. He was also a confirmed monogamist, and as he was also a jealous concealer of his own life, we know nothing of his sexual intimacies. Apparently there was no other woman than his wife.

A solid Jewish heritage weighed upon him. He was not a believer, but he had a strong feeling of community with his people.[12] He had breathed in the ancient atmosphere created by a despotic God and a somber religion in which sin was the main idea. It has been rightly said that "never a people had been so much in love with virtue as those puritans who seemed to have stepped out of the Old Testament without any interruption of Catholic centuries."[13] Freud, who knew Greek and Latin, was not insensitive to the charms of ancient times, but his soul did not vibrate to the sound of the flute or the sistrum or the drum in the temple of the goddess of love, Aphrodite. He was an austere man who, though sensing as nobody else had the Greek tragedy, *Oedipus*, nonetheless did not share in the crude language of Aristophanes (450–385 B.C.), the great comedian. He was, after all, a Jew.

It is undoubtedly a paradox that a son of this ascetic people was the one to astonish the world by demonstrating the universality of incestuous feelings. Freud disclosed this erotic world, but with cold prudence.[14] Obscene words, with their ability to call forth seductive images, were prohibited to him. "His descriptions of sexual life," points out his disciple and biographer, the English psychoanalyst, Ernest Jones (1879–1958), in *Life and Work of Sigmund Freud* (1957), "are so barren that many readers have considered them arid and lacking any warmth."[15]

Sandor Ferenczi (1873–1933), Freud's greatest pupil and the one to make "of all analysts his disciple,"[16] understood better than his teacher the therapeutic value of obscene language. The Hungarian psychoanalyst believed that it was necessary to confront the patient with "dirty" words. Only in this way was it possible for him to genuinely release repressed affections. Ferenczi, who was prudish in his own writings, provides us with instructive examples in his essay *Uber Obszöne Worte* (1911).[17]

One example deals with a hysterical 23-year-old patient. The young woman was able to listen without embarrassment to extensive sexual explanations put forth in strictly scientific language. Furthermore, she could talk uninhibitedly about sperm, the egg, the sexual organs and their union. Her peculiarity was that, since she was a child, she had to close her eyes when she sat on the toilet! Ferenczi then had a happy intuition. Perhaps she closed her eyes so as not to read the obscene words usually decorating public restrooms? The young woman, upon hearing the interpretation which drew her attention to the familiar *graffiti* in her memories, was filled with shame. And thus, for the first time in the therapy, she finally had access to her deepest and most hidden erotic memories.

Equally interesting is the example of a homosexual patient. During long hours in treatment he had resisted uttering the word *fart*. He tried to avoid it with allusions, foreign words, and euphemisms. It was only when he could overcome his resistance and utter the dreaded word that he had the possibility of understanding emotionally the complex world of ideas associated to the *ass* and to its voluptuousness, which for obvious reasons was so important in his love life.[18]

Certainly, we do verify day after day Ferenczi's experiences. An adolescent who came to me, for example, could not utter any obscene words during his psychoanalytic sessions. His inhibition was absolute. One day when I said *cunt,* he put his hand on his forehead and nervously told me: "Doctor, when you say that word I can see it here." His comment left no ground for doubt. The obscene word had provoked in him a visual, moving representation of feminine genitalia. Hallucination is a distinct quality of all these words. Analyzing his difficulty in saying these words took us to the deepest source of his neurosis. "Dirty" words as well as dreams are a true way to the unconscious. They provide, like the old roads built by the government, wider and more perfect access to the hidden world.

The boy was forbidden a full erotic life. He could not experience it with all the splendor and intensity that obscene words evoke. He could refer to sexual pleasure only through veiled allusions. To mention coitus with his girlfriend, for example, he said, "Yesterday I 'did it' with Cristina." This description aroused no affective response in him. He talked about sexuality but did not feel it. His moral conscience tolerated eroticism at the cost of frigidity.

Henry Miller (1891–1980), the American writer, shrewdly expressed this lexical limitation of civilized man in his *Tropic of Capricorn* (1939):

> What is unutterable is *fuck* and *cunt*, pure and simple, they only must be mentioned in limited editions; otherwise, the world would be shattered into pieces. Bitter experience has taught me what supports the world is sexual relations. But, the real *fuck*, the real *cunt* seem to contain an unidentified element which is more dangerous than nitroglycerine.[19]

Let me stop for a moment and summarize. Thus far, I have sought to make these points: first, that dirty words are "dirty" because they are obscene; then, that they are obscene because they truly reveal the sexual life that should not be shown in public; and, finally, that all of them are endowed with an almost magic, hallucinatory force, and this is one of their most certain qualities.

II

Psychoanalysis has thoroughly probed the psychic mechanism of hallucinations. To hallucinate means to perceive the nonexistent. It is a mistake in our judgment. A typical example might be an oasis in the desert that extends itself before the eyes of the thirsty and exhausted man. Another example is Anna O. (1842–1925), the patient who led Freud to some of his initial psychoanalytic discoveries, and who used to see imaginary snakes and skulls. It is a frequent symptom of the seriously disturbed patient. Actually, we are used to considering it as characteristic of a particular state: madness.

We assume that only the crazy have hallucinations. However, a brief consideration of our everyday life confronts us with the limitations of this belief. Indeed, do not all of us suffer regularly from hallucinations? After all, what else are dreams? The weirdest, most wonderful, most absurd, or most frightening events parade before our eyes and we do not hesitate to consider them as real—at least while we sleep. In this respect (yet not only in this) we are all a bit insane. Therefore, if we understood the cause of these commonplace hallucinations we surely would be able to understand them all.

Let us see, then, where our wisdom ends. Why do we dream? Imagine a soldier in the midst of battle. Suddenly, a bomb explodes very close to him, but it does not hurt him. He has a great shock and he blacks out. After several days he starts having fits. Awake, he hallucinates the explosion; moreover he lives it again, very painfully, in his dreams. The bomb blasts again! Why? When sleeping we break our psychic contact with the outside world, and in so doing, our attention decreases, as does our ability to control the stimuli surging throughout our minds. In this way, disagreeable, and even terrible, memories, which we had managed to keep in check during the day, crop up into consciousness through dreams. We revive experiences we thought we had forgotten. The past re-enters with such overwhelming force that we cannot repress it. We do not feel it to be our own, but rather as queer and alien. It now belongs to the outer world. The hallucination has happened. This, in any case, is the theory.

We are made in such a way that we always consider

as belonging to the outside world painful inner stimuli that we cannot suppress. Although, of course, there are not only memories, but also thoughts and wishes. Plato (427–347 B.C.) the Greek philosopher, at the dawn of our civilization had sensed this truth (see *Republic,* IX, 571). Our dreams feed on our repressed longings. The ordinary man only dreams what the criminal carries out:

> As you very well know, in these moments that part of the soul dares everything, as if it were loose from every shame and every sensibility. It does not hesitate to rape its mother with the imagination, or to give itself to anyone, be it man, god or animal; no murder draws it back, no nourishment does it abstain from; in short there is no insensible or shameless deed it is not ready to carry out.[20]

During the night our buried desires escape from their prison and threaten to recreate awesome and sinister scenes. Asleep, we cannot reject them, and then we fall into a traumatic situation. (This name is given in psychoanalysis to every situation in which there occur overwhelming quantities of upsetting stimuli.[21]) Consequently, we hallucinate. The beauty and happiness that are often experienced while dreaming are simply the result of our last and desperate subconscious efforts to mask this dreadful landscape. Yet, sometimes, the traumatic force of these innermost personal experiences is so powerful that it overwhelms the awake individual as well. Then we daydream. This is the hallucination typical of psychosis. Thus, the origin of hallucinations is always the same: what is repressed traumatically invades our consciousness.

3

THE WAY OF THE MILK

"Flesh in blossom, oh my breasts
How rich in voluptuousness you are!"
PIERRE LOUŸS
(Les Chansons
de Bilitis, III, 1894)

I

How beautiful women's breasts are! Their voluminous spheres have moved men in all times. The most inspired, deeply felt verses were offered to them. In the *Song of Solomon*, the lover sings to his loved one's beauty:

> Thy two breasts are like two young roes that are twins, which feed among the lilies.[1]

And even more enraptured:

> How fair and how pleasant art thou, O love, for delights! This thy stature is like to a palm tree, and thy

> breasts to clusters of grapes. I said, I will go up to the palm tree, I will take hold of the boughs thereof: now also thy breasts shall be as clusters of the vine. . . .[2]

Breasts have been immortalized through sculpture and painting. Their power is so great that even during the Renaissance, under the censuring eye of the church, they succeeded in revealing themselves, full and delicious, by way of depicted images of the holy Madonna.

Every man rediscovers his first love in female breasts. That little boy who, caressing and determined, introduces his small hand into his compliant mother's dress searching for the loved breast, (for example, as depicted in the painting, *The Virgin and the Child*[3] by the Spanish mannerist painter, Luis de Morales [1510–1586]) follows a route consecrated by instinct–a true manifest destiny. The same boy, now an adult, will also continue to look for the breast. Following the track of the past, perhaps, he may press the breast morbidly, much like the mischievous god of love in the twisting, *serpentinata* figure in *Venus and Cupido* (painted by the refined Florentine, Bronzino [1503–1572]). And while enjoying it, with ecstasy, he will revive the pleasure of being a child again–with mother's *tits*!

Evidently, man's attitude towards female breasts has reflected the vicissitudes of his shifting appraisal of women, in general, during the long course of our civilization. The old exaltation of her body, "What a back and arms I saw and touched! And the shape of the breasts, made for caresses!" (Ovidio, *Amori*, I, V, 17–25), was followed by Jewish disdain, "More hateful than death I consider the woman, whose heart is bristled with traps and tricks . . ." (Ecclesiastes 7:26); as well as Christian rejection, "It would be good for the man not to touch the woman" (Corinthians 7:1–2). In the Middle Ages she was already the personification of evil. The pious Saint Odon of Cluny (879–943) was obsessed by the anguishing question:

> But if we refuse to touch dung or a tumor with the tip of the finger, how can we desire to kiss a woman, a bag of dung?[4]

Nevertheless, within the church itself, there were some strange and eager advocates of the disturbing female protuberances. Among the Jesuits of the 17th century, there were some individuals who supported the right of man to touch woman's tits in the *rebus amoris*. Their names were Benzi and Rousselot, but they were also known by the witty and obscene name of *tits* theologians.[5]

II

Tit, thus, is a typical obscene word–the first on our list. It is a word common in Spanish, Portuguese and French, as well as dialectically known in other Romance languages. It is a word that children use expressively. Although similar words exist in Greek, Celtic, and certain Germanic languages, they represent parallel creations, and there is no reason to believe that tit was taken from any of them.[6]

In spite of its being such a widely-found word, it is impossible to say *tit* in adult, educated language. In Victorian England, for example, the use of the word *breast* to refer to that part of the anatomy of birds was banned because it reminded one of women's breasts. Bosom had to be used instead. Women had bosoms but never *tits*!

However, how ridiculous it would be to hear a mother with her full breasts, saying: "I have to give my son the bosom." It would be far-fetched because mothers have *tits* and it is *tits* that they give to their children! Can it be that the prohibition against uttering the word is due to the maternal atmosphere that it brings to mind? Can it be that the word evokes nostalgia for mamma's *tits*?

Sucking mamma's *tits* is something most of us have done, and we all, with more or less violence, have had to renounce that intimacy because mother herself took it away from us. Afterwards a mantle of silence covered our love history forever (no other prohibition is more peremptory than silence). Such silence was also a successful invitation to forgetfulness. Who as an adult mentions the *tits* to the mother? Who, after weaning, has thought of them without anxiety? Who has looked at them without being embarrassed? The well-known and sweet infant *rendezvous* always ends up being a forbidden date: extremely forbidden, because sucking *tit* is an incestuous pleasure, and thus desire must give in to the taboo, must surrender to repression.

Finally, to add insult to injury, one day a sibling arrives. What a torment, then, to watch the intruder drinking from the warm source of pleasure that was ours! The pain becomes absolutely excruciating as the mother, in ritual manner, says: "You have to love him a lot. Mamma will love you both." (Imagine arriving home, finding your wife with her lover sucking her *tit,* while she is uttering the same comforting words to you.) Undoubtedly, the history of the child's early sexuality is one of pleasures and detachments, joys and renouncements. Desire is never exhausted. It remains forever ready, waiting for the proper occasion. At a given time, it returns from repression, and the inextinguishable longing for the *tit* takes over with all the strength of a postponed, untamed, indomitable instinct.

III

One of my psychoanalytic patients told me about his first encounter with "the clusters of grapevine."

He was seventeen. She was a girl of the same age, tall, with an inexpressive face and a bit on the chubby side. She was a maid who lived in the home of a neighbor. Together, they agreed to have a furtive meeting. One night, he called on her, entering the house from the terrace. The girl was waiting for him in bed, and immediately he went over to her, unbuttoned her blouse and loosened her bra. And then, in the midst of intense excitement, there appeared before his astonished eyes two ample tits. As in a Fellini film, they revealed themselves, flooding his visual field. He could not believe it, but there they were. He could look at them, touch them, suck them. Then a sudden feeling of shame overcame him. He felt like a child! Nevertheless, the die was cast, and the heavy masses of flesh were falling softly into his welcoming hands. He squeezed them almost with incredulity, and in his mouth he took the big, smooth tit. What an immense pleasure! He was indeed a child. And how not be so? Every man feels like a child when he can fully yield to this enchanting regression to the past. For sucking the tit is always a return. So much so that the girl, aware of her inexperienced lover's frenzy, whispered in his ear with maternal solicitude: "Are you hungry, my love?"

IV

Not only is the word *tit* forbidden, the word *suck* is forbidden as well. However, it is the best term to describe the lover's mouth movement over the tit. It is used with complete correctness, for sucking means exactly: "to draw milk or liquid into mouth by making vacuum with muscles of lips" (*Oxford Dictionary*). But the prohibition goes right on. Thanks to chaste and boring psychoanalytic books, we have become accustomed to the scientific definition: "suction" (it means exactly the same). So men do not *suck tits* anymore, now they suction the bosom!

For the adult male, to *suck tit* is a longing that is seldom satiated. In Veronese's voluptuous painting (1528–1588), *Mars and Venus Joined By Love*[7] the goddess of love tenderly covers the immortal warrior's shoulder with her left arm, while with her right hand she squeezes her *tit* from which a thread of milk flows, delicious food that the hirsute, muscular, and virile god is about to enjoy. Well then, this is precisely the appetizing culmination usually forbidden to mortals! Only a married man can sometimes share with his son the milk in the full breast of his wife. But this is not common. The infantile, intimate, and indissoluble pleasure of the *tit* together with the *milk* is a pleasure man often denies himself. And yet desire for such pleasure always remains, hidden and seeking outlet. Imagination never rests. It looks for new ways of expression and almost without pretense it finds that expression in art.

In Giambologna's (1519–1608) sculpture, *The Fountain of Neptune* (1563–1567),[8] in Bologna, the eternal fantasy is manifested in the form of a robust, plump, and sensual nymph, who movingly opens her legs to mount an enormous fish with her powerful and noble thighs, while at the same time generously squeezing her prominent tits and lavishing the longed for, dancing fluid. Even in ancient Egypt, during Pharaonic times, popular poetry offered up simple, erotic wisdom in harmonious verse. Thus we observe, in writings from Memphis of Thebes, circa 1500 B.C., an unabashed awareness of the amorous value of *tits* and their rich content:

> Are you leaving because you want to eat?
> What are you, then, slave of your belly?
> Are you leaving to cover yourself?
> But I have sheets on the bed!
> Are you leaving because you are thirsty?
> Then take my breast
> What it contains is enough for you.[9]

The milk in female breasts is a tenacious and persistent motive in man's thought in all ages. In 1453, for instance, at a party given by the Duke of Burgundy, it was decided that for the guests' joy, a young and beautiful women would show her full *tits* out of which abundant milk was flowing.[10]

And still another example: The Greeks, with their wonderful and sensual imagination, provide us with the myth of the origin of the "Milky Way." In short, Hera, wife of Zeus, the Master of Olympus, whose honeymoon lasted 300 years, breast-fed Hercules, the future hero. The little boy, foreshadowing his energetic character, bit and hurt her *tit,* and so the milk that spilt inextinguishably over the wound formed the Milky Way in the firmament, "the way of the milk." Thus, since then, for our solace, the warm food runs its route between the stars in the sky.

Finally, I might mention briefly a patient of mine. He was a 40-year-old man, and he used to visit the poor neighborhood in the city looking for mothers who were breast-feeding their children. Upon finding them, he approached them and, after a courteous prologue, offered them money for sharing the child's food. This agreement was one he succeeded in making many times.

V

But, what happens to the woman? Obviously, as a child, she has also *sucked tits* and enjoyed them as much as the man, but she will have to forget about them forever unless she, as an adult, seeks them in her girlfriends, like Lesbos' daughters of Mitilene Island in ancient Greece. In fact it is precisely during this warm repetition of the intimacy between a mother and her offspring, as pointed out by one of Freud's first disciples, the Polish psychoanalyst, Helene Deutsch (1884), in her *Psychology of Women* (1944–1945), that the inverted woman finds "the utmost satisfaction in homosexuality."[11]

Bilitis, heroine of the French writer Pierre Louÿs (1870–1925), was overwhelmed by an ineffable voluptuousness when her charming lover Manasidika disclosed her tempting *tits*:

> Gingerly, she barely drew her gown and offered me her warm and soft breasts, as a couple of small living turtledoves are offered to a goddess.

> Love them! she said. I myself love them so much! They are two darlings, two little children. When I am on my own I find joy in them. And I play with them and I make them have delight.
>
> I bathe them in milk. I cover them with flowers. My delicate hair which I use to dry them is loved by their little nipples. And I caress them, tremulous, and I put them to bed on fine wool.
>
> Since I will never have children, be their creature, my love and as they are far from my mouth, kiss them for me.[12]

This sweetness is depicted repeatedly in paintings. We witness it when, during their shared bath, Gabrielle d'Estress delicately caresses the Duchess of Villar's nipple (in the 14th century painting of Jean Cousins, the Young[13]); when wet female bodies promiscuously share *The Turkish Bath*[14] (Ingres [1780–1867]); and when two beautiful naked women sleep together, one of them resting her beautiful head on her girlfriend's pink-nippled breast in *The Dream*[15] (Courbet [1819–1877]).

The fact is that Sapphic love has deep roots. Besides it assumes different faces. It was a widespread Greek custom. Indeed, the term "sapphic " derives from Sappho, the lesbian poetess from 6th century Greece. Not only Plato praised homosexual love. Naucrates, the philosopher from Alexandria, also saw something captivating in the union of two young women, as long as both of them preserved their femininity, kept their hair long, and did not use fake elements imitating the stronger sex.[16]

Psychoanalysis has tended to support the kind philosopher's intuition. Except for cases in which women adopt an openly masculine attitude by using some *ersatz* or penis substitute, the most delicate forms of female homosexual love have a tender, child-like aura. The *ars amandi* becomes exhausted in a maternal intimacy.

Helene Deutsch is eloquent:

> The remark often heard from little girls–"you are little and I am big"– can be realized in a situation that allows the girl to do to her mother what she had done before to her.[17]

Then she specifies:

> The preference of the oral cavity for sexual activities of homosexual women is based on this relationship with the mother. Most investigations have overlooked the frequency with which homosexuality assumes this form, which can be referred to as a reprised desire towards the mother. These women meet their beloved homosexual objects in a mother–daughter relationship more or less consciously acknowledged.[18]

As it happens, only a minority of women choose to follow the path of lesbianism. Most women naturally choose men. In men, they do not find the longed-for *tits* but Nature's luxurious compensation–man's *cock*!

So, here we have a new "dirty" word, one that also has a powerful affective impact and a great hallucinatory potency. Undoubtedly it is one of the most severely proscribed terms on the list of obscene words. Let us draw our attention to it. The etymology of the term *cock*, the most widespread nickname for penis, is interesting and simple: the erect comb of the cock, that lustful bird, was the inspiring image.[19]

Linking the word *cock* to the disturbing word *suck* gives rise to a new, vigorous, frankly exciting phrase: *to suck cock.* The popular psychoanalytic term for referring to this erotic experience–namely, *fellatio,* the commonly used Latin equivalent–provides only a pale and sentimental image of reality. For a woman, to *suck cock* is a habit as inveterate as it is joyful. It constitutes a magnificent substitute for the maternal breast, and as such it gives her a pleasure usually forbidden to the man who *sucks tit:* she receives from the *cock* warm and thick fluid.

The sexual act of *sucking the cock,* is considered by Freud, in "An Infantile Memory of Leonardo da Vinci" (1910), as follows:

> Investigation also shows us that this situation so implacably condemned has an extremely innocent origin. It is not but the transformation of another one in which all of us have been happy and pleased; that is, that situation in which as breast fed children we hold our mother's or wetnurse's nipple with our mouth and suck from it.[20]

The father of psychoanalysis also included a curious hypothesis. He thought that when a girl discovers the udder of a cow, which "in its function equals the nipples and for its shape and position in the lower belly reminds us of the penis," the conditions are established for displacing associatively from top to bottom and from women to men, the pleasure of sucking.

However, it is not indispensable to look at the popular mammal to make up this exquisite fantasy. It is rather the observation of the father's or some older brother's cock which makes this imaginary transit easier. The girl is driven towards this fantasy quite naturally. Her first love, just like a man's, was her mother, yet her destiny is not a woman but a man. She will normally abandon mother to seek father. From the *tit* to the *cock* is her typical sentimental itinerary. A woman's love life is more complex than a man's. She will discover her father only after she has enjoyed a precocious homosexual intimacy with her mother. In the later unconscious identity of the *tit* and the *cock,* the images of her two first loves (mother and father) will be merged, and both will live on everlastingly in her soul.

The desire to *suck cock* has been tenaciously manifested throughout the ages. As Freud points out:

> . . . the inclination to hold a man's member with her mouth and suck it, an act which has been included by bourgeois society among the repugnant sexual perversions, is, nevertheless, very frequent among contemporary women and as ancient paintings and sculptures prove, it was so among those ones of a past time as well. . . .[21]

Nowadays, pornographic magazines reproduce this modality of *fare l'amore* prolifically and in detail, but representations of this amorous habit have a long history. They were very popular in India. Scenes of *Auparishtaka,* or oral union, can be found in the sculptures of numerous temples of Shaiva and Bhuvaneshwara, near Kattak in Orisa, built around the 8th century.[22] They were also depicted on glasses and amphores in ancient Greece,[23] on the lamps and tiles in Pompey[24] and in the stunning pottery of Moche culture in ancient Peru.[25]

During the Renaissance, the painting, *The Three Ages*[26] by Giorgione (1471–1510), who "enjoyed love matters" and "lived in love with life, beautiful women and music,"[27] depicts a young flutist about to play his instrument which has been introduced between the legs of a man who is lying almost naked (to play the flute is a typically obscene allusion). The peak of the swan in the fleshy lips of Leda, depicted in *Leda and the Swan* (1529)[28] by Michelangelo (1475–1564), and the same topic in the ambiguous and provocative painting by Giorgio Vasari (1511–1574),[29] further testify to the persistence through time and space of a truly immortal desire.

VI

In sum, then, we can see that the scandalous words *tit* and *cock,* as well as to *suck tit* and *suck cock,* take us back to the world of childhood: to mother, her *tit*, and the candid pleasure we had when sucking it. We have also found out painfully that that innocent and idyllic picture was transformed by incestuous prohibitions into an accumulation of disagreeable stimuli; in short, into a traumatic and hallucinatory situation.

A true metamorphosis took place – and what a cruel transmutation of values it produced! The sweet pleasure of being breast-fed became an indecent and disgusting act. Instinct, of course, has always been the same; it is our opinion of it that has undergone a change. This is our real finding, the richest fruit of our efforts: evil is not in the instinct expressed in "dirty" words but in our minds, it is not in life but in the soul. How right German philosopher, Friedrich Nietzsche (1844–1900), was when he firmly stated that we do not need a moral interpretation of Nature but a natural interpretation of morals!

"Dirty" words constitute an authentic trigger of deep memories and ancient passions. They not only awaken dormant desire but also prohibition. They revive the great incestuous conflict and provoke trauma and hallucination. That is why they should never be written or uttered. Their free and indiscriminate use, mainly among close relatives, would inexorably give rise to incestuous fantasies and reminiscences. Yet, as Freud demonstrated to the world, only the integrity of our memory guarantees our health. To deny our infantile sexuality is a vain goal. As if bad memory could cancel the past! But taboo is clumsy and obstinate, and of course, it is beyond reason. Repression is its sole, primitive gesture, and so, repression is called forth. For, in the final analysis, incest is always the *ultima ratio*, the ultimate reason for prohibition. It is the "unidentified element more dangerous than nitroglycerine,"[30] which Henry Miller talked about and which lurks behind all unmentionable words. All the words that can evoke incest are condemned so as to proscribe it from consciousness. They are, indeed, the *dirty words.*

4

WE ARE BORN AMONG FECES AND URINE

"Undoubtedly man feels ashamed of whatever might remind him of his animal nature."

SIGMUND FREUD
(Prologue to a book by John Bourke, 1913)

I

Prohibition does not rule over all dirty words with even-handedness. Condemnation hangs over them with different intensity. Obscene words that mention organs or excremental functions can be more freely employed. They have been used not only in vulgar language but the most well-known literary works have employed them too. *Graces and Disgraces of the Asshole* (1626), for instance, is the title of a work by the great writer and humanist, Francisco de Quevedo y Villegas (1580–1645), one of the most outstanding writers in Spanish literature. However, it is clear that in our daily life it is not possible to speak spontaneously and openly about this hidden part of our anatomy, nor about what comes out of it.

This is one of the great hypocrisies of civilized life. We are all suffering, like the "perfect angels" from the final scene of *Faust* (1808–1831), by J. W. Goethe (1749–1832), from "the earthly waste which is painful to bear."[1] Thus, only in the most extreme cases do we allow ourselves to refer to those indecent features of our humanness. Even so we do it with great reticence. In antiseptic fashion, we speak of the anus, and further along the alimentary canal, the rectum. We say we have to *defecate* or *move the bowels*, we refer in medical tones to the *feces*, and we blush when *flatulence* occurs. Perhaps we should make up a private code like the women imagined by Freud. They had gone on an excursion to the countryside and said they would pick up flowers when in fact they just wanted to satisfy their physiological needs.[2]

All these linguistic mannerisms are, as Freud pointed out in *Jokes and Their Relationship to the Unconscious* (1905), due to repression:

> We grant culture and good education a great influence on the development of repression and we admit that those factors carry out a transformation of the psychic organization – which can also be a hereditary trait and therefore, inborn – owing to which sensations that would otherwise be perceived with delight become unacceptable and are rejected with all our psychic energy.[3]

Civilization with its restrictions constrains us from placidly enjoying our instincts. It transforms pleasure into disgust, condemning besides, the authentic scatological language. (The term *scatology*, incidentally, comes from the Greek *skor, skatós*, which means excrement.) Thus, less well-educated individuals typically have greater sexual freedom. They are openly coarse and have no need for masking concupiscence with euphemisms. Among higher social classes, on the other hand, "impudence is only accepted within a funny context."[4] The use of "dirty" words reveals a less prudish and more vigorous spirit. The creator of psychoanalysis always thought that there exists a tension between culture and sexual instinct.[5] He also believed, for this reason, that the proletarian erotic life was freer than that of the bourgeois.[6]

In keeping with this scheme of things, there are those who have wittily suggested that mankind may be divided into four classes, depending upon their use of excremental language. Thus, those who employ the term *wee-wee* belong to the highest and most refined class. "One has to be quite a gentleman to use that word."[7] Those who say *pee* belong to the class immediately below. It is a word preferred by "employees, army men's widows, the families of small investors and by middle class in general."[8] Further down the social scale, we meet the third group comprised of people who employ the verb *urinate*. These are plain, kind, and unaffected people who live by their manual work. Finally, those who say *piss* belong to the lowest level; they represent the most populous class, composed of less educated people.

All that is scatalogical is taboo. This is the reason why words referring to excremental things have to be uttered in mute, dull, almost vague tones. Clear, descriptive, "dirty" words are absolutely banished. In fact, civilized human beings make up a dishonest brotherhood that presumes and pretends men and women have no *ass,* do not *fart,* ignore what a *turd* is and of course never, ever *shit.*

II

These contemptible words have an old genealogy: *piss, ass* and *fart* derive from Middle English *pissen, ars* and *farten*; and *shit* from Middle Dutch *schite.* In spite of their illustrious past, we cannot imagine that great figures commit the human acts these dirty words represent. For example, Greek gods have been represented in art in the most diverse situations and adventures since the Renaissance, yet never have they been depicted in the act of defecating. Neither has the holy Christian family nor the Jewish god. The taboo is so powerful that if a citizen of our civilized world obscenely stated in public that the President of the Republic, or the Commander in Chief of the army, or the Pope regularly sits his *ass* on the toilet and *shits,* he would be censured for having broken a taboo–just as if he were a native from Galla de Ghera, or a Sakalavo or a Guajiro, or a Zulu. The terrible rule cannot be broken with impunity.

The hallucinatory strength of obscene words would at once induce in the audience the visual image of the high dignitary satisfying his needs in an indecorous position. And that would be unacceptable. It would remind us of the animal nature of these great figures. Indeed, their greatness resides, in part, in the denial of such animal traits.

The perception of greatness is born from our submission to taboo. Grandeur is always a fiction; a deep-rooted adulteration of human nature. A man who *shits* and *pisses* can never be a god. This was the dreadful doubt that haunted one of Freud's patients (known as "The Wolf Man"). This patient began his treatment by offering to have anal intercourse with Freud and *shit* on his head; and he further stated that during his childhood he kept wondering whether Christ had an ass and also *shit*.[9]

The Catholic Church accurately perceived this inverse relationship between *shit* and greatness. Since the 10th century it instituted the stercoraceous chair as part of the ceremony on the Consecration Day of a Pope. The term stercoraceous derives from the Latin *stercus*, which means excrement. The chair, placed before the door of the basilica, was no more than a majestic, portable toilet. Its aim was to inculcate the virtue of humility in the Pope ("to be seated on the throne" is precisely a well-known excremental allusion). The openly stated motive of the distinguished seat was:

> Stercoraria sedes, in qua creati pontífices ad frangendos elatos spiritus considerent unde dicta.[10]

This is translated as:

> Stercoraceous chair where Pontiffs sat soon after being raised on the canopied throne, to deflate arrogance, hence its name. (This custom incidentally, was abolished by Pope Leo X who occupied the canopied throne from 1513 to 1521.)

The same subversive capacity of consecrated values, typical of excrements, is comically portrayed in the *Farce de Maître Pathelin* (1480) (author unknown), a masterpiece of the French Comedy. In a wise rebuke to the vessel that collects urine, it is said:

Presumptuous urinal, why are you offended?
For having obliged women to squat on their legs?
Before King and Queen we humbly bend our knees
but the very same Queens are obliged to bow before
you.[11]

Frankness as to scatological matters is always iconoclastic; it debunks idols. As Napoleon said, nobody is a hero to his own valet. And inasmuch as excrements are without exception an asset common to all men, the sincere acceptance of them as part of our human condition undoubtedly constitutes a step in the direction of democracy.

III

In all ages, stercoral matter has been erotically inspiring and quite unorthodox pleasures have been associated with it, such as this truly salacious scene. The characters were a patient of mine and his lover. She was a lustful woman with wide sexual experience. Had she lived in ancient times she certainly would have worn the dress of the courtiers of Frigia (a district in Asia Minor), which exposed the so-called 22 areas of the skin where caresses are irresistible. As for my patient, he was a man always seeking new sources of lascivious inspiration.

One day, excited though ashamed, he schemed up a new pleasure: he would piss her in the mouth. They had never done anything like that before but he had confidence in himself. Although inwardly he felt perverted, the mere fantasy of it awoke immense passion in him. He held back from urinating for several hours and then went to look for her.

The young woman worked at an office building

where each floor had a shared restroom. Upon meeting her, he at once persuaded her–no difficult task. She always let herself go in a mixture of salaciousness and childish openness. They headed right to the bathroom, their mutual excitement increasing with the risk of being seen. Immediately, he asked his docile mate to kneel down, and then introduced his almost flabby cock into her mouth. He tried to constrain his erection so as to be able to piss better but the girl, possessed, could not stop sucking his cock. It was beyond her own will! Only with great effort did he achieve the necessary continence. After a brief but intense wait, little by little, first drops and then short spurts of urine started flowing, which soon became an abundant, continuous and almost endless stream. The young woman, upon feeling the warm fluid enter her throat, buried her nails in his thigh while her face burned with passion. Afterwards, when he had stopped pissing, she began to lovingly suck his cock, now hard and powerful, until another different but equally longed for liquor also flooded her.

When ecstasy vanished, my patient was overwhelmed with remorse. He was a pervert! An abnormal! He escorted his lover home without even mentioning what they had just experienced and made up his mind to forget all about it. He succeeded in doing so only for a few days. Then he started yearning more and more strongly for the same adventure. A week later, almost as if complying with a liturgy, he repeated the same scatological ceremony.

IV

Literature also provides us with some impressive excremental scenes. *La Philosophie dans le Boudoir* (1795), the posthumously published book written by the famous and obscene Marquis de Sade (1740–1814) during the frenzied times of the French Revolution, offers us some of these secret fruits. The lustful Madame de Saint Ange, one of the heroines of this coarse writer, with loving devotion instructs her charming and young disciple, Eugenia, in the ways of debauchery:

> My husband was already old when we got married. Since the very first night he warned me of his fantasies assuring me that he would not hamper mine. I swore to obey him and we have always lived in the most delicious freedom. My husband's whim consists in having me suck his cock and while bent over him with my buttocks over his face heatedly sucking the liquor from his balls, he wants me to shit into his mouth! . . . And he swallows it![12]

To Eugenia this is an extraordinary fantasy. But Dolmancé, the main character in the play, and a man who happily collaborates in the young lady's education, further adds:

> No fantasy can be thus qualified, my dear; all of them are part of nature which takes pleasure, when creating men, in differentiating their likes as well as their faces. We should not become more astonished of the diversities placed on our inclinations than of those placed on our features.[13]

Undoubtedly the scene is repugnant. To *shit* into the mouth! We feel that this is an abominable perversion, even more abominable than that of my patient. But Dalmancé alleges, with philosophical dispassion, that it simply constitutes a natural disposition; *de gustibus non est disputandum* (there's no accounting for taste). The plot is astounding and immoral, but is it possible that these pleasures that seem so monstrous to us are nothing more than simple and naive wishes? Can it be that the immoral Dolmancé is right?

V

Only an unbiased analysis of the facts can provide us with an answer to this question. Let us look into it, then. The gathered data on the use of human and animal excrement in the religious, medical, and everyday life of human beings, throughout history, is truly amazing.

The Zuni Indians of New Mexico, for instance, after participating in a traditional ritual dance, greedily drank urine out of a pot. When this same dance was performed in a large plaza, it was considered honorable to eat man's and dog's excrements as well.[14] As another example, we note that the Parsi of ancient Persia, after getting up from bed, rubbed their faces and hands with the urine of cows. They also believed that upon delivering a baby, Parsi women should drink urine; and so too should children at the time of being dressed in the symbols of their faith.[15]

The Feast of the Crazy in continental Europe and in Russia was also closely related to the Zuni's dance. It consisted in a chanted mass attended by clergymen whose faces were painted in black or covered by an ugly mask. At a certain time, and in front of the priest celebrating mass, many of these clergymen approached the altar and ate black sausages – obvious substitutes for feces. (The translation of the French word *boudin* is black sausage, and also excrement.) Once mass was over, participants riding in carts loaded with filthy matter enjoyed themselves by throwing it upon the surrounding crowd. The Feast of the Crazy was no doubt a pagan survival within the Christian Church. In France it disappeared after the Revolution, in other areas of Europe during the Reformation.[16] For our purposes, it may be considered as just one more poignant reminder of man's coprophagic instinct.

Coprophagy, to get fed with *shit* and *piss,* is actually a widespread habit. In insane asylums the tendency of many patients to eat their excrement is well known. Of course, it is also true that these strange *gourmets* do not live only in asylums. The Roman Emperor Commodus who ruled from 180 to 192 bore the same weakness. It is said that he often mixed human excrements with highly refined dishes and did not abstain from tasting them.[17] This is not an exceptional instance. The same tastes have been shared by primitive tribes from Florida, Texas, east of the Rocky Mountains, California and Lake Superior in North America, to the Negroes of Guinea, the savages of Australia, natives of Siberia, Cochinchina, Central Africa, some devoted men from India and aborigines of the Patagonia. And this does not exhaust the list of these bizarre diners.[18]

The excrement of great religious personalities has also been highly valued nourishment. In former times, eating the *shit* of the Great Lama of Tibet was a consecrated form of worship. Feces were carefully collected, dried and employed in different ways: as seasoning, as sniff-powder or as medicine. Tartars and Japanese, apparently also relished his manure.

This coprophagous custom, however, is not exclusive to Lamaism. Anyone interested in studying the discussions that Christian believers have had on the subject of the Eucharist will be surprised to discover the great importance that *shit* has had in this matter. It even gave rise to the coining of a new term, *stercorist*; the name given by the Catholic Church to those who considered that the Eucharistic bread was subjected to digestion and to all the other processes that food undergoes. This well-known theological discussion started in 831. It is interesting to point out that in the *First Gospel of Jesus Christ Childhood*, which seems to have been accepted as authentic by those who followed the religious doctrine of gnosticism, as well as by Eusebius, Athanasius, John Chrysostom and other Church Fathers, it is possible to find revealing quotations regarding the extraordinary powers of the diapers worn by the Christ child, and also the water in which he was washed. Apparently, the excrement of the Nazarene was considered efficacious in achieving miraculous cures.[19]

In the Jewish religion these scatological, savory dishes are not unfamiliar either. It is known that God ordered Ezekiel (Ezekiel 4:12) to mix manure into his light meals. For 390 days he should eat barley, wheat, and millet bread cooked underneath human excrements. The prophet resisted this mandate and so God said to him:

> From now on instead of human excrements I will give you oxen excrements to cook your bread with.[20]

However, this moving act of stercoral piety is not comparable to the unusual devotion that Romans and Egyptians felt for excrement. They even imagined deities whose role was to protect latrines and their visitors. The Roman goddess of latrines was called Cloacina and she was one of the first Latin deities, though apparently this was picked up from the Pharaohs' lands. This worship was not a privilege unique to European or Asian countries. In America, the ancient Mexicans also had a coprophagous deity. She was called Suchiquecal, mother of the Gods, and habitually she was represented as if about to eat excrement. There was also a Goddess of dung called Tlacolquani, who presided over the pleasures of love and flesh.[21]

The homage rendered to *fart* has not been any the less. In some countries farts have been accepted with religious devotion. Among Egyptians, the *Fart* was a deity represented as a crouched boy pushing to *shit.* However, the Syrian cult to Belgafor was even more striking. This ritual was excremental and obscene: "They uncover the anus before him and offer him dung." *Farts* had, then, the character of true oblations; they were gifts to their god.[22]

Among the Greeks flatulence was considered a good omen. For the Romans it was the opposite which induced Cicero, Latin statesman and philosopher, to commit his illustrious eloquence in making amends for the *fart,* which he considered an innocent victim oppressed by the civilization of his time.[23]

Christians, too,, were not alien to this deeply felt respect. The German, Martin Luther (1483–1546), the main promoter of the Reform in the 16th century, attributed to the *fart* greatly dissuasive powers, as evidenced by his story of a woman who "Sathanum crepitu ventris fugavit" (with her flatulences, made Satan run away).[24]

Last but not least, it is worth mentioning the great importance that both urine and stools have had in medicine in all ages. They have been a most persistent pharmacopoeia. Asclepiades (124–46 B.C.) Greek physician, was the first to advise on the use of human excrement. This was already an ancient custom in the East, especially in Egypt. Hippocrates (460–357 B.C.), the father of modern medicine, recommended these remedies as well. This medication was so widespread that Aristophanes called physicians *skatóphagous*, excrement eaters. Eskines of Athens, Jerapión of Alexandria, Dioscorides (1st century A.D.), Galen (131–201), and Sexto Placito (4th century) are classical writers famous for their stercoral medical prescriptions. One of these medicines, for instance, indicated for the cure of tuberculosis, consisted in mixing the dry shit of an adolescent with Attic honey:

> . . . the boy, however, had to be fed on vegetables and a somewhat salty bread made of yeast and baked in a small oven. He should also be moderate when drinking wine.[25]

Diseases considered curable by the use of human *shit* and *piss* were manifold: headaches, insomnia, dizziness, madness, melancholy, gout, seizures, paralysis, epilepsy, eye inflammation, cataracts, otitis, nasal bleeding, caries, pleuritis, spasms, intestinal worms, syphilis, sterility, and the list goes on. Excrement was a true panacea.

We have come to the end of our odorous journey. In sum, we have discovered, by noting the scatological customs of the most diverse human communities, that our aversion to excrement is not due to our nature; rather, it is the result of a distortion. *Piss* and *shit* have been recognized and worshipped in all places and times. They have been considered delicious dishes and attributed prodigious properties. They have also been religiously worshipped. Civilization with its progressive establishment of strict moral prohibitions has helped promote our contemporary and artificial response, full of disgust and repugnance. The evidence speaks out clearly: Our deepest attitude towards excrement is not that of scorn but that of love. Evidently, Marquis de Sade's hero, Dolmancé, was right after all.

VI

One of the great merits of Freud's work has been to make us aware of the primitive aspects of ourselves; that is, the infant within each of us.

As Freud fascinatingly observes:

> Restricting ourselves to what we have learnt about excretory functions, the main discovery made by the psychoanalytical research is that the child, during the first stages of his development normally recapitulates all the attitudes successively shown by the human race with respect to evacuation; the first of which was quite likely assumed when the *Homo sapiens* stood up on the earth mother.[26]

The child is absolutely shameless with his excrement. For example, he thrives when curiously smelling his stools. Arthur Rimbaud (1854–1891), the French symbolist poet, tells us how, when he was young, in the suffocating summer days, his mother would not let him go out to play.

> . . . il était entété à se renfermer dans la fraicheur des latrines; il pensait là, tranquille et livrant ses narines.[27]

> (Stubbornly he locked himself up in the coolness of latrines, there he quietly contemplated, dilating his nostrils.)

Yes, the great pleasure of the little savage is to tarry, and enjoy *shitting.* It is a pleasure that will accompany him throughout his life and in some cases, as with the Austrian musician Wolfgang Amadeus Mozart (1756–1791), the enjoyment will be strong and even unabashedly acknowledged. The artist went through a time in which he seemed to be fascinated by the excretion of *shit.* In a letter to his mother he celebrated *farts* in prose and poetry.[28] When he was 21 years old he wrote to his cousin, Anna Thekla, truly coarse letters. In one of them, dated November 5, 1777, he tells her:

> I wish you good night but before shit on your bed.[29]

And in another letter written on November 13:

> I have been shitting, that is how you say it, for almost twenty two years through the same hole which is not in the least worn out.[30]

Or, to cite another man who seems to have savored scatological pleasures, we recall the Irish writer, James Joyce (1882–1941), author of *Ulysses* (1922). He described and classified farts with the accuracy of an expert. Nostalgically, he wrote his girlfriend, Nora Barnacle, on December 8, 1909:

> That night you had your ass full of farts, my sweet heart, and I got them out, they were fat, hurricane-like, fast, tiny, cheerful backfire, and many brief and disobedient farts which ended in a prolonged gabbing of your asshole. It is wonderful to fuck a farting filly if at each charge you get a fart out of her. I am sure I would recognize Nora's farts anywhere. Youthful sound unlike those wet, noiseless winds I imagine fat married women release. Sudden, dry and stinking like the one a shameless girl would expel at night to enjoy herself in the bedroom of a boarder. I

> hope Nora does not stop laying farts on my beard so that I could recognize its odour.[31]

But to return to the little savage, the eternal inspiration from the unconscious of all these adult pleasures, we note that not only does he show great interest in expelling and smelling excrement. He also likes to play with them. He stares at them, touches them, and like the imaginative Marquis de Sade, he eats them!

All of the child's behavior shows not only a manifest love for stools but also a fondness for his farts. And why not? Stools have first been inside his body, before emerging slowly and pleasantly into daylight. They are his first piece of work, the first production that carries his own trademark! Indeed, do not many adults still secretly watch their copious *shit* in the toilet!

The child though loves not only his own excrement but also other people's, above all his father's and mother's. His stercoral pleasure is selfish as well as social. He wants to share this pleasant intimacy with his parents. He invites them to, or visits them in, the toilet, which is his favorite meeting place. He wants to enjoy communally these agreeable moments; he asks for, even demands them! And this promiscuous pleasure will survive barely masked in his adult life.

John Gregory Bourke (1843–1906), a student of the scatological rites of human beings, provides us with a revealing anecdote. He recalls a great Magnifico of Venice who was ambassador to France during the Renaissance. The high dignitary was one of those individuals who never renounced this infantile, excremental sociability. It thus happened that one day, while granting an audience to a noble character, he obliged him to stay along with him in the toilet as a gesture of particular courtesy. And later, when he felt the need to sit down again on the toilet, he generously called him back![32]

Men and women have always found pleasure in relieving themselves while in amiable company. Among the Romans, for example, in the times of the satiric poet Martial (42–104), this sort of comradeship was not contemptible at all.[33] The Swedes have a revealing axiom: *Svensk man pissar inte ensam* (a Swedish man does not *piss* alone).[34] Among Italians, a well-known *marchigiano* proverb runs: *"Chi non piscia in compagnia o fal il ladro o fa la spia"* ("He who does not *piss* in company is either a thief or a spy"). Finally, we note that everywhere people enjoy reading in the bathroom. This, too, is a legacy of the same infant pleasure; after all, don't we say that reading is "good company"?

In short, our affable excremental society with our parents is perpetuated into adulthood. It constitutes the unconscious model of our adult sociability, the rich inspiration of the noisy female meetings, the untiring engine of the ritual coffee-talks of men, and the source of all the different ways of gathering expressed in the warm gregarious life of man.

VII

The scatological intimacy with our parents is undoubtedly one of the great pleasures of childhood, but like all first fruits of infantile sexuality, it must be renounced. Excremental lust is an incestuous pleasure, and like all such pleasures it, too, cannot escape prohibition.

The obscene words *ass, shit, fart, to shit, to piss*, provoke strong and rather prohibited erotic sensations. They generate a true shock. That is why they are so vivid and why they cause hallucinatory sensations. Were they to occupy a place in our everyday language they would arouse powerful representations of the excremental organs and their secretions, as well as of the persons who have and produce them. We would find ourselves hopelessly wrapped up in a disturbingly erotic atmosphere.

No, it is not possible to use "dirty" words. They are too truthful. However, often we need to talk about our shameful physiology. How can we do it then? In general, we take one of two paths: we use scientific terms, or we use the same euphemistic words as we resort to when talking about children's products or organs: for example, *wee-wee* and *dirt* when referring to *piss* and *shit*; or *weeny* and *bottom* when describing the *penis* and *ass*. These euphemisms conjure up for us the small sizes and scanty products of children. In a word, we are allowed to think freely about the naked human body provided that it is the body of an infant or child. Adult sexuality, or more precisely, the sexuality of Mom and Dad, is what is proscribed.

This new knowledge enriches our characterization of "dirty" words and we can formulate it as follows: obscene words always stand for the adult anatomy. The outcome of this moral zeal is always neurosis. Freud neatly described this phenomenon:

> The power that hampers the woman, and to a lesser degree the man, from enjoying the manifested obscenity is that one we call "repression." We recognize in it the same psychic process that in severe pathologic cases keeps entire complexes of feelings bound to all their derivatives aloof from consciousness. This process has

> been shown as one of the main factors in the pathogenesis of the so-called psychoneurosis.[35]

The psychoanalyst thus seeks to put an end to repression, and the liberation of anal and urethral pleasures is one of his defined purposes. Ingenious procedures have been devised to help the sick person abandon his inhibitions. The psychoanalyst, Georg Groddeck, an unruly character and dear friend of Freud's, was in the habit of suggesting to the incredulous patient that for the sake of research he make the experiment of allowing:

> . . . urine to run along his arms and thighs since otherwise he would not be able to believe that the child thrives on this. Besides, he considers those adults, who from time to time get such a pleasure, perfid, believing they are antinatural, vicious and sick. The only sick aspect of this pleasure is fear. Try it, what is hard is to do so without feeling inhibited.[36]

His suggestions, besides, were not limited to these warm, golden baths. He also invited his patients to roll about the *grumus merdae*; he predicted the return of an ancient pleasure:

> And not to speak of making shit and lying on it. To grasp the idea of doing such a thing takes whole days of pondering and only three or four of those, who, eager to know, wished to investigate under my supervision the development of the unconscious dared do so. But they confirmed what I was stating.[37]

Saint Augustine (354–430), saw in the body and in sensuality the greatest sin and source of all evil. To strengthen his argument he formulated a renowned phrase: *inter feces et urinam nascimur* (among stools and urine we are born). Excrement was unquestionable proof of the wickedness of our flesh. Several centuries later, Voltaire, with greater sagaciousness and spirit, recognized instead that evacuation of excrement is as necessary for life as is nourishment. He did not hesitate to state that as much industry and power is needed to defecate "as to produce the semen that gave birth to Alexander, Virgil, Newton, and Galileo."[38]

VIII

The taboo imperiously demands repression of incestuous desire. Therefore, it is necessary to exorcise the evil and magic power of "dirty" words, but when banishing the feared voices, emotions bound to them are also chased away. Then Eros, the naughty and playful god of love, deeply suffers because he enters an antiseptic and cold world; a world of scientific terms and infant allusions; a world without passion.

The consequences are severe because, as psychoanalysis has thoroughly shown, only those who are unfrightened by their past incestuous longings are able to love intensely. By not repressing their infant memories or reminiscences, they do not give up passionate feelings attached to them. The excremental passion is an important ingredient in desire.

The unconscious longing for that early and infant scatological promiscuity with his parents is what strongly excited Mellors, the well-known gamekeeper created by D. H. Lawrence (1885–1930) in his widely read novel

Lady Chatterley's Lover (1928). Addressing his lover, Connie, Mellors exulted:

> "An' if tha shits an' if tha pissis, I'm glad. I don't want a woman as couldna shit nor piss." Connie could not help a sudden snort of astonished laughter, but he went on unmoved. "Tha'rt real, tha art! Tha'rt real, even a bit of a bitch. Here tha shits an' here tha' pisses: an' it. I like thee for it. Tha's got a proper, woman's arse, proud of itself. It's none ashamed of itself, this isna." He laid his hand close and firm over her secret places, in a kind of close greeting. "I like it," he said. "I like it! And if I only lived ten minutes, an' stroked thy arse an' got to know it, I should reckon I'd lived one life, see ter! Industrial system or not! Here's one o' my lifetimes."She turned round and climbed into his lap, clinging to him. "Kiss me!" she whispered.[39]

5

CRUELTY AND SUBMISSION

"While castration can be a very important unconscious idea of punishment in masculine masochism, it is not in the least the only one, as analysts supposed for a long time. Together with or independently from the idea of castration, more grotesque ones appear, like that of being used as a woman by another man, being raped or fecundated."

THEODORE REIK
(Masochism in Modern Man,
I, Chapter X, 1949)

I

Dolmancé learnt from a friend of mine about the superb member that, as you know, I have. He engaged the marquis of V . . . to invite me to have dinner with him. Once there, it was necessary to exhibit my member. At first, curiosity seemed to be the only motive but suddenly, a beautiful ass offered to me from which I was begged to enjoy, made me see that only pleasure was the object of this examination. I warned Dolmancé of all the difficulties of such an enterprise and nothing intimidated him. "I could bear a catapult, he told me, and you will not have the glory of being the most respectable of the men who perforated the ass I'm offering you." There was the

> marquis fondling, touching, kissing everything that one and the other were uncovering. I seem . . . I want some arrangements at least: "Do not do that"–said the Marquis–"for it would make you lose half of the sensations that Dolmancé expects from you; he wants you to break it, tear it . . ."[1]

In this way, The Knight, Madame Saint Ange's brother, tells us about his first meeting with Dolmancé. In his luxurious description, authenticity is achieved through the use of dirty words. This is unquestionable. Let us imagine for the sake of mere academic curiosity, what would have happened if instead of asking his *partenaire* to "break and tear his ass," Dolmancé had invited him, in psychoanalytic terms, to have anal coitus with him! It is evident that the scene would have rapidly lost its power. Only a weak and almost hypocritical allusion would remain of the disturbing heat. This is so because obscene words give the sexual picture not only a powerful affective reverberation but also a genuine description of motives. Dolmancé does not long merely for something which enters his ass but something which enters it, tearing and breaking it. He does not want just pleasure but painful pleasure. He does not want to have anal coitus. He wants *his ass to be broken!*

It is precisely this tremendous sincerity that gives the amazing Marquis de Sade his permanence and singularity. Indeed, the psychiatrist, Richard Freiherr von Krafft-Ebing (1840–1902), founder of the modern study of sexual pathology, immortalized the Marquis in his book, *Psychopatia Sexualis* (1886), coining with his name the specific psychopathology of finding pleasure in cruelty: sadism.

To break the ass is the "dirty" word that draws our attention now.

II

The ass possesses a mysterious attraction. "What a beautiful ass you have!" Lady Chatterley heard her lover say this, as she was being tenderly caressed. After the deeply felt tribute, the gamekeeper added:

> Tha'rt not one o' them button-arsed lasses as should be lads, are ter! Tha's got a real soft sloping bottom on thee, as a man loves in is guts. It is a bottom as could hold the world up, it is![2]

Sometimes it is true that these voluminous rear cheeks of a woman's body arouse amorous desires of kissing them and biting them softly, thus showing that they evoke the other two sweet prominences of a woman: her tits. It is undisputable that in front of a kneeling woman who frankly and provokingly offers her superb ass, as in the famous Pompeian frescoes in the House of Vettii,[3] a definite yearning for penetrating violently is awakened in man. The splendid plenitude of a woman's ass is always irresistible. That is why female opulence has always been a motive exalted in literature, as in this epigram by Martial (*Epigrams,* XI, 100):

> I do not want, oh Flacco! a lover who is like a thread in whose arms a ring can be put on with a skinny ass and sharp knees. . . .

The desire to possess a woman anally – in the "Italian way" as described by Benvenuto Cellini (1500–1571), the turbulent Renaissance goldsmith – is always ready to spring forth in the passionate man. The fact is that each sexual organ has a singular power to arouse instincts. The tits arouse tenderness; the ass, sadism.

The strong charm of the female bottom is a constant note through time and space. For example, the Hottentot Negroes, who live near the Cape of Good Hope, especially admire those women whose asses protrude in an extraordinary way. It is said that one of their most beautiful women ever had such a developed rear that she could not stand up once she had sat down; to do so she had to creep until she got to an incline. Moreover, this female peculiarity is also found in other black tribes. Men from Somalia in West Africa choose their women by making them stand in a line side by side and picking the one whose ass protrudes the most. Nothing can be more horrible to these men than the opposite shape.[4]

The "rear part" of Venus also had many admirers in ancient Greece. Greek young women, just like contemporary ones, publicly competed to see who had the most beautiful thighs. Even a temple in Syracuse was dedicated to the Callipyge Venus, which means the goddess of thighs.[5]

However, there were times when the pleasure of "enjoying from Venus' rear" was harshly condemned. Christianity definitely contributed to that. As early as the 6th century in France, the monk, San Benito de Aniana (750–821), seriously warned believers, in his *Summa Benedicti*, that "to know" one's wife anally was a mortal sin. In time, this prohibition reached extraordinary heights. In the 16th century, there were women who made their husbands forgive their adultery under the threat of denouncing them for attempting anal intercourse. Such a whim could cost a man his life![6]

Of course, the punishment for male homosexuals was not less. In the Middle Ages, they were led to the scaffold. Dante (1265–1321) in his *Divina Commedia* (1304–1318) unmercifully condemned them to the eternal torment of his *Inferno*.[7] In the 18th century, homosexuals were burned at the stake.[8]

Moral condemnation, even though implacable in its punishments, has always been very scanty in its reasons. It has been claimed that sodomy is blameworthly because it is against the "natural order,"[9] only what leads to conception is natural in the art of love. This is a strict interpretation that is hardly accepted by any lover! After all, what child can be born out of the passionate kisses in which the tongues cross each other untiringly? Which pregnancy can be reasonably expected as a result of sucking a tit, sweetly introducing one's tongue into an ear, or softly biting a slender neck? Undoubtedly, Nature has wider and more varied erotic purposes than those prescribed by any neat catechism.

No less narrow and inconsistent is the hygienic argument that it is unclean to introduce the prick where shit is. This is obviously superficial. As Freud pointed out, this reasoning is not more consistent than that given by "hysterical girls to explain their repugnance towards male genitals: the fact that they serve for urine expulsion."[10]

Nevertheless, it is undeniable that this ancient passion is based on a conspicuous feature of human behavior, sometimes angelically denied: cruelty. The pleasure of inflicting or bearing pain, physical and moral—this is its true essence.

III

Freud provided us with still a further explanation. He believed that *poedicatio*, sodomy among men, as in the case of Dolmancé, was inspired by the anal penetration of women. For him, male homosexuality had its model in the fantasy of anally possessing a lustful female.[11] In this regard, the Marquis de Sade, Donatien Alphonse Francois, thought the opposite way:

> I confess my weakness. I agree that there is no pleasure preferable to this. I adore it with either sex, but I accept that a youth's ass gives me more voluptuosity than that of a young woman's. They call *bugger* the man who gives himself to this passion but when one is a pederast, one must be so completely. To coit women through the ass is to be only half a pederast: it is in men where nature wants men to fulfill this fantasy, and for men she has given us this taste.[12]

Freud's opinion is seductive, but de Sade's point of view also has a certain accuracy. For instance, the obscene phrase, *ass-fuck*, is in fact a typical masculine image, a commonplace in male conversations. It constitutes a clear manifestation of triumph and violence: "I am going to *have his ass*." Or of irritated expectation: "That guy wants *to have our asses*." Or what about provokingly showing and offering one's genitals to another man while holding them with one's hand on the fly?

Perhaps no other expression so dramatically shows the deep and hidden purpose of victory and domination of one man over another. In the deep roots of every virile conflict the fight is always to conquer a woman. Being the most macho means enjoying the female, and subduing the rival in a feminine way. This latent motive is ready to feed unconsciously any disagreement with its inexhaustible strength. How else can we explain that whatever the declared motive of dispute–economic ambitions, political passions, family quarrels, or sport enmities–the same obscene image is crudely employed. Undoubtedly, every conflict among men awakens in the root of the soul, behind the manifest complaint, this sexual matter. Hence, the popularity and omnipresence of this dirty word.

Thus, the idea of *having the ass* seems to have been born in a men's world. Freud *versus* the Marquis de Sade, who is right?

IV

As a matter of fact, the origin of the solid link between anality and sadism still constitutes an enigma for psychoanalysts.[13] What is the reason why the ass appears so tied to cruelty? There has not been a sure answer so far. However, this erotic affinity is a fact of everyday observation. Indeed, do we not often hear parents threateningly say to their children: "I'm going to spank you on your bottom?" Furthermore, who has not had, more than once, the irresistible impulse of kicking somebody who is bent down, daringly exhibiting his ass? Daily experience is undoubtedly eloquent.

Even from ancient times we can trace this almost inextricable *liaison* between cruelty and the ass. For instance, whips have been one of the oldest methods of punishment. Ancient Egyptians who untiringly carved their stories and legends on the walls of their buildings, depict in their bas-reliefs severe guards whipping prisoners and slaves. Moses, the Jewish hero, had to escape from the country of the Pharaoh for having killed one of these whippers.[14] This punishment was also known in Jewish holy law. The delinquent had to lie on the ground, and in the presence of a judge, receive blows from a stick (though never more than 40).[15] Among Romans, the naked man was held by his neck with a fork and then whipped.[16]

Within Christianity, flagellation has existed almost from the beginning. It flourished at the end of the 11th century when it was common for parishioners to be whipped on the premises next to the church. Saint Dominic (1170–1227) in the 12th century considered that a thousand whips were equivalent, as punishment, to the recitation of ten penitential psalms. By the middle of the 13th century, flagellation was regularly practiced during endless demonstrations of the faithful, demonstrations that were led by the priests themselves. Sometimes, even whole towns participated in these bloody displays of piety.[17]

Of course, these ferocious practices did not meet an end in that obscure age. Punishment by whipping continued until recently. For instance, in the old German penitentiaries, prisoners were flagellated with devilish frequency, upon entering and leaving the prison and often every Friday.[18] In England, flagellation was abolished only in 1948. In this country, whips were very popular in the 19th century, during which they became a true fad at home, at school, in brothels, and in prisons.[19] As usual, punishment was even crueler in the military. There, sadism reached its pinnacle.

On a visit to the *Victory*, Admiral Nelson's old flagship, shocked guests could see a sailor condemned to punishment by whip–a whip that he was forced to braid himself.[20] So great was the passion for the whip among the British that it became known on the Continent as *le vice anglais* (the English vice).[21]

The history of the vicissitudes of this cruel punishment provides us with an insight regarding one more dirty word, or phrase. Namely, it seems likely that whipping is nothing but a masked way of *having someone's ass.*

Let us analyze the facts. We are accustomed to thinking that whipping is given on the bare back and that the instrument of punishment is a whip brandished by the executioner. This idea is not wrong, but it is not totally accurate either. It is rather the result of a long evolution. Originally, the back was not the object of this sadistic attack, nor the whip its tool. In fact, the ass was the original target of these cruel fervors; and the instrument of punishment was not a flexible object but a rigid one.

The flagellator always set his eyes upon the fleshy human buttocks. In England, during the Victorian euphoria for flagellation, this was the favorite place. Extensive and detailed literary pieces were published on this exciting pastime. In this respect, the book attributed to a young Breton writer, Hughes Rebell, deserves special attention. The book had a generous title:

> The Memories of Dolly Morton, the History of a Woman's Participation in the Struggle to Free Slaves. Account of Flagellations, Rapes and Violence which Preceded the Civil War in the United States, with Curious Anthropological Observations about the Radical Diversities in the Shape of Female Ass and the Way Different Women Bear Punishment.[22]

In brief, what the *Memories* recount is the tale (or perhaps, tail) of Dolly, an orphan who travels to a place in Virginia, right in the heart of the slave states. There, she becomes the lover of the owner of a great plantation, Randolph, a man who enjoys flagellating her with whip and birch sticks, and then making love to her.[23]

Of course, the preference for human buttocks as a target of punishment was not exclusively English. In Jesuit schools on the European continent, for instance, punishment still flourished at the end of the 18th century.[24] Every day, undisciplined children were taken to the corrective "father" to be publicly punished. One after the other, they were held still by two friars while the "father" pulled their trousers down and delivered blows ranging from 10 to 200.[25] This was an old custom among religious congregations. In the 6th century, Benedictines had to kneel down or pull up their tunic and display their glutei so as to be whipped by their superior.[26] Up to the 18th century, throughout Europe, whipping was the punishment usually meted out to whores, adulteresses, or witches who had been spared from the stake.[27] And for 1,000 years in Rome, people used to come and see the ferocious show in which a pontifical executioner made the asses of the damned bleed.[28]

In 1915, whips were used in German prisons. The criminal's hands and feet were tied to a rack,

> so that his buttocks are kept tight; then, twenty-five to seventy whips are striken on the naked buttocks with a cane, a pizzle, a leather whip or a rod, being possible to vary the maximum number. . . .[29]

There was no unanimity of criteria in Germany as to whether prisoners should be whipped on their naked buttocks or with their clothes on. In Saxony, for instance, the ass had to be bare, but in Prussia and Oldenburgh, the matter remained unsolved.[30] During the same time in the United States, whippings were administered to prisoners in Cannon City, Colorado, and there too, the prisoners were also undressed before punishment.[31] And in general, whips on the naked buttocks of men as well as women have always been considered a severe punishment.[32]

The symbolic character of *having someone's ass*, which is typical of flagellation, is even more evident when we realize that the original whip was not a flexible instrument made of leather or rope as it is today, or heavy chains as preferred by the very cruel Roman emperor Caligula (12–41) but instead was an elongated device made of rigid material.[33] In short, a typical symbol of the penis.

At this point, the knowledge of genital symbolism is of great help. It was one of Freud's most interesting findings, although many humanists and anthropologists had already noted it in their studies of ancient and primitive cultures. "Every long-shaped object, that is, sticks, tree trunks, parasols, and umbrellas (the last two for their similarity to erection when being opened), as well as all long and pointed weapons, knives, daggers, pikes, are representations of the male genital organ."[34] Thus, fig tree branches or stalks–used as whips in the Targelian feasts of Athens in honor of Apollo and Diana–as well as the straw bunch, birch rods, hazelnut clubs, or canes should also be considered as such symbols.[35]

A hint of sensuality always can be found in the practice of whip punishment. In Southern Delaware, the picket where the condemned were tied, usually a column made of stone or brick and mortar (typical phallic representation), was painted in red. When tied to the column as if embracing it, black men would say they were hugging "red Jane,"[36] an obvious reference to the hidden sexual submission. A similar masochistic fantasy was very popular among British sailors who were often subjected to flagellation. It was said that the man tied to the cannon (another well-known symbol for the penis) in order to be whipped, was about to "marry, hug or kiss the artilleryman's daughter."[37]

Thus, we can summarize our new knowledge. It is evident that a phenomenon Freud discovered early in his adventure through the world of the unconscious takes place in the brutal punishment: namely, displacement. Wishes and feelings do not remain bound forever to beings and objects they once represented. They undergo different vicissitudes and often search for new targets. This is, of course, an unconscious process; yet a true transposition of emotions takes place. A unique characteristic of this phenomenon:

> Such an idea is that, within psychic functions, something must be distinguished (the strut of emotion, the magnitude of excitement), something which has all the attributes of some quantity–although we have no means for measuring it–something susceptible to increase, decrease, displacement, and discharge, which spreads along mnemonic traces of representations as an electric load on the surface of the bodies.[38]

So this is the transposition that has occurred from *having someone's ass* to flagellation. A process of displacement has taken place through time. Cruel impulses unconsciously changed their direction. They shifted from the ass to the back, and from the cock to the cane or rod or whip. Moreover, in some cases, as in the story of Dolly Morton, whipping and coitus followed one another without interruption, thus revealing their fundamental affinity. The same consummation was also common in Brazil during the time when slavery existed. The young slave was sometimes forced to submit to the whims of his master. It was the so-called "bastonada" during which a number of blows with a cane on the buttocks of the helpless Negro was followed by penetration with the other "stick," also hard but fleshy.[39]

V

Anal submission is not only carried out under the mask of flagellation, it also takes place openly. In fact, together with castration, they constitute the two characteristic ways of emasculating the defeated or imprisoned man. Through castration, a man loses his distinctive attributes; and through sodomy, when penetrated by another man's cock or any of its substitutes, his becoming a woman is completed.

Emasculation as punishment is a horrible, long-standing custom. It can be found in the old Assyrian penal law, in Persia, Abyssinia, Greece, Rome, and in Europe during the Middle Ages. The whole of human history is afflicted by the stigma of this dreadful way of punishing.[40] It was often meted out as a punishment for the crimes of rape and adultery. The explanation was simple: the delinquent had to be punished on the part of the body with which he had committed the fault. Sexual offenders were not the only recipients of this punishment. It was also administered to other types of criminals and other individuals, including captured soldiers, as well. So, evidently, the reasons for this cruel and irrational behavior should not be sought within conscious motives but within the obscure, unconscious reasons even ignored by the executioners themselves.

By applying psychoanalysis to the study of history, the English psychoanalyst, Edward Glover, in *War, Sadism and Pacifism* (1933) has shown that in every war, there are cruelties that clearly exceed tactical needs.[41] During the periodic holocausts in which men destroy one another, the same ways of debasing the defeated man are obsessively repeated. This takes place whatever the causes of the war: hurt national pride, religious ardor, or economic voracity. The warrior wants to degrade and humiliate his opponent, and castration and anal rape are the supreme ways of doing so.

In Ancient Egypt, for example, a soldier would cut the dead enemy's cock and take it to the corresponding scribe to have it recorded to his credit.[42] Castration was also practiced among Abyssinians on the enemy dead; it was known as *sellaba.* Each warrior could only castrate those he had beaten in an open fight.[43] This punishment knew no rank. Even emperors were submitted to it. The conspirators who killed Caligula did not forget to run their swords through his genitals.[44] Also the testicles of those executed by hanging often were nailed to a pike and shown triumphantly.[45] In Haiti, one of the favorite punishments inflicted on slaves was *brûler un peu de poudre au cul d'un nègre* (stuffing gunpowder into the rectum and causing it to explode) a torture in which the idea of having someone's ass reached its highest development.[46]

As another example of such practices: in Arezzo,

Italy, in 1502, a riot burst out against an oppressive city commission. One of the victims was undressed and hanged. Then, somebody put a burning torch into his ass, perhaps satisfying a universal fantasy that knows no time, no race, and no nations. The joyous mob baptized the body with the name of *il sodomita*.[47]

In more recent times, we have seen in the chronicles of the war in Algeria how both sides, the French and the Arabs, rarely gave up the powerful passion of cutting off the dead soldier's genitals and stuffing them into his mouth.[48] Even as recently as 1982, newspapers around the world published a disturbing photograph in which a group of English soldiers imprisoned by Argentine troops during the Malvinas (Falkland Islands) War were obliged to lie down on their stomachs with their asses up in an evident posture of anal submission.

Now, let us stop and ponder for a moment. Since all the punishments detailed above involve sexual abuse, even though the crime or the war had nothing to do directly with sexual offenses, it appears that man always winds up sexualizing every conflict. If this is so, what then is the real trophy men unconsciously seek? It is not difficult to figure it out. Erotic rivalry between men can only have a single origin. *Cherchez la femme!* Seek the woman! She is always, consciously or unconsciously, the motive for quarrels among men.

VI

Our findings do not conclude here. It is plausible then that these deep-rooted and widespread ways of submission are not only manifested in man, but also his near ancestors:

the animals. And indeed, observation of animal behavior confirms our expectations. Among animals, the intimate link between sexual rivalry and submission is revealed with absolute transparency. Says Charles Darwin (1809–1882), in *Origin of Species* (1871): "In the animal kingdom, the possession of the female seems to be as a result of combat rather than seduction."[49]

The law applies to both aquatic and terrestrial animals. Even the most shy among them start terrible fights in time of heat. Also, acts of submission have a curious similarity in all their fighting rituals; for example, those of hares, moles, squirrels, beavers, guanacos, seals, sperm whales, deer, elephants, and wild bulls. Darwin's statement is, in addition, readily verifiable: the fierce dispute among dogs for a sexually pleasing female can be seen rather commonly. Only the bravest and most powerful one enjoys her.

Similar scenes are discovered in the life of another much loved animal: the horse. Horses that freely live in herds seldom gather in groups larger than twelve. Stronger males have two to eight females in their harems, along with their respective offspring. Colts, in turn, separate from the family when at the age of three they lose fondness for the herd's leader. They then live without females within a group of young males who have suffered the same fate. All of them have a leader that while not having sexual intercourse with them, nonetheless subordinates, controls, and disturbs them as if they were females (as usually happens in human groups formed exclusively by men).[50] They wander in gangs, still too immature and weak to challenge the dominant horse who keeps all the females to himself. They wait for their turn. The chief's old age or weakness will give them the cherished opportunity. Meanwhile, the lustful females invite the impetuous males by adopting the seesaw position, urinating, lifting their tails, opening and closing the lips of the vulva, and showing the clitoris.[51]

Actually, the language of tails is most interesting. When a horse (or dog) is afraid, it hides its tail between its legs. It is significant that we use the same phrase "to go away with the tail between the legs" to describe the behavior of a frightened man. Undoubtedly, this is not the only expressive affinity we intuitively notice between our emotional responses and that of animals. Actually, they are multiple and varied. Thus, just as horses gather behind the leader when facing great danger, and lift their tails to shit,[52] we are used to saying that a coward is "one who shits in his pants." The deep affective identification with our zoological relatives is manifested in these spontaneous popular phrases. The power of the instincts creates an undisputable solidarity between us. We understand animals because we are animals too.

This is an instructive fact, one which was noted early on by Freud in the psychoanalysis of his patients. There exists a language of the organs both in animals and in human beings. Body organs express their desires and fears in both species. That was true in the famous case of the patient known as "The Wolf Man." When at the age of 1½ years he saw his parents fornicating in a dog-like position, he reacted to their loving moment by shitting on the bed.[53] Freud did not hesitate to consider this event as a sure sign of the child's feminine tendencies; he had identified himself with his mother. The explanation was obvious. If he had identified himself with his father, he would have urinated instead of defecating. Anal passivity prevailed over penile activity. Thus did the Wolf Man's organs show a capacity for psychic expression beyond mere physiological needs. Of course, that was not a weird or unusual event. On the contrary, it was an ordinary experience. A patient of mine who was suffering from a poor erection and early ejaculation always wanted to defecate when arriving at a motel with his girlfriend to have sexual intercourse.

Body organs make their voices heard, and these voices are rich and expressive. The language of fear and submission is especially interesting for our purposes. In horses, for instance, chattering teeth is a sign of fear (also used in relation to human beings), as is retrieving their tails and also defecating. There is an unexpected gesture, however, that has even surprised experienced researchers: horses show their asses as a sign of submission![54] Is it necessary here to remember that the obscene phrase *to offer the ass* is also one of the favorite ways of describing a man's submission to another?

VII

The Austrian naturalist and Nobel Prize winner, Konrad Lorenz (1903), states in his book, *Das Sogenannte Böse* (1963), that these typical gestures of submission are also clearly observed in the wolf.[55] The aggressive life of the ordinary wolf is very suggestive, and in fact, it has a rich and popular literary tradition. Dante called it the *bestia senza pace* (beast without peace), and we all remember how it frightened children in the tale of *Little Red Riding-hood*. Nevertheless, it has also been the legendary protector of abandoned children, such as the she-wolf that breast-fed Romulus and Remus, Rome's founders. It is one of the most intelligent mammals on earth. Its struggle for power is very illustrative for our study. When in packs, wolves are led by a lead wolf, but fidelity to the leader is very unstable. Sometimes, confrontations end in death, for the wolves bite each other until they rip arteries and veins. If not killed, the beaten wolf will lie down offering its neck to the winner (human beings, instead, would kneel down offering their hands joined by the palms as a sign of passive surrender to the victorious warrior). Then, the animal that eagerly looked for its rival's neck before, avoids the fatal bite, smells it, growls, flashes its teeth, and finally pisses beside it![56]

Wolves have definite hierarchies. When a wolf with lower rank approaches one with higher rank, it does so with its ears drawn back and, as among dogs and human beings (the army private in front of the powerful general), with its tail between its legs. In this sense, the obscene phrase, *he wrinkled his ass in fear*, expresses with great eloquence this animal tendency in our human responses. Undoubtedly, in order to put its tail between its legs, the wolf must also contract its ass. In other words, if we still had tails like our ancestors the apes, we would also wrinkle our ass to put the tail between our legs.

After this initial gesture of submission, the weaker wolf crouches before its superior's snout and licks it rapidly. Finally, if the dominant male keeps its arrogant position, the threatened wolf lies on its back and urinates while the other smells its genitals.[57] Thus, through urinary incontinence, the animal displays another noticeable similarity to man. The prematurely ejaculating man is also incontinent, and for the same reason: the impotent man is, unconsciously, a terrified man.

These attitudes of submission are often repeated in many mammals. The custom of offering the ass among males is common among our closest ancestors, the monkeys.[58] It is mainly observed in papions, a type of South American monkey, and in young mandrills from the west coast of Africa.[59] In this regard, Lorenz tells a convincing anecdote:

> I once saw a momentary real fight between two robust sacred cynocephalus (*Papio hamadryas*) at the zoo of Berlin. A moment later, one of them was running away and the winner was chasing it until it was finally cornered. Not seeing a way out, the beaten ape resorted to a gesture of submission and immediately afterwards the winner went away with stiff legs and an arrogant look. Then, the defeated one angrily ran after the other insisting on showing its ass until the stronger monkey acknowledged the submission while boringly mounting it and making some effortless copulation movements. Only then, the beaten baboon seemed to calm down and convince itself that its rebellion had been forgiven.[60]

The whole life of our hairy, ugly ancestors is instructive. Charles Darwin, inspired by the customs of superior apes such as gorillas, thought that primitive man lived in small hordes dominated by the oldest and strongest male who jealously hoarded his females, most of them sisters and daughters.[61] He also killed, castrated, or expelled challengers who dared make a pass at these females. When opposing him, his sons, full of hatred, either fought until they could beat him or submitted themselves shitting in fear, wrinkling or offering their asses, as a sign of humiliation. The ass, no doubt, has always been the favorite language of submission.

VIII

In the history of human culture the importance of the father within this primitive horde is immeasurable. His dreadful punishments currently survive, hardly altered, in initiation rituals that still take place in many primitive societies. They are but traces of that horrible progenitor's ferocity.

Rituals occur, for instance, when youngsters reach puberty. That is not a coincidence. Puberty is the time when sexual life can start to be fully enjoyed. That is why it is the moment chosen for initiation, and thus the ceremony usually consists of a token mutilation: for example, the initiated ones are circumcised. It is not difficult to perceive the purpose of this anguishing ritual. Its message, based on *pars pro toto* (the part for the whole) is the following:

> Now you are an adult. From now on, you may enjoy women. But, beware! Some are ours and some forbidden. We now cut your prepuce. It is a warning. If you break the law, we will castrate you.[62]

The primitive father used to castrate his sons who became sexually bold with his women; old men who currently circumcise just mutilate and threaten. This is the progress achieved after thousands of years. Castration and circumcision are mere variations of the same theme. For this reason, Theodor Reik (1888–1982), Austrian psychoanalyst and Freud's *protégé*, could state, in his book *Ritual* (1914), that circumcision always represents an equivalent of castration, being in addition the most effective way of incest prohibition.[63]

Even though circumcision is the most conspicuous way of ritually instilling obedience, it is not the only way. As we have already noticed, anal subjugation is its regular mate. As a matter of fact, among natives in Australia, during puberty rites, youngsters were circumcised and also had their asses penetrated.[64]

IX

The power of that protohistoric father can still be found not only in remaining initiation rites and rituals. His shadow is projected even over the most sophisticated products of our civilization. It tenaciously, though slightly concealed, persists in them. This is the case of religion.

Freud was thinking of that fierce leader living ages ago, when he stated: "Father God had formerly existed in flesh and bone on earth, exerting his dominant power as chief of the primitive human horde."[65] The head of the horde has been the unconscious model of the gods that arose in historic religions. This is not, of course, a totally original finding of psychoanalysis. The idea of primitive man creating gods in his own image is very old.

In the 6th century B.C., the Greek, Xenophanes from Elea, author of philosophical poems, pointed out that:

> There was not and there will never be a male who knows about the gods with certitude. . . . Mortals think that gods have been born and wear dresses and have voices and appearance like them. But if oxes and lions had hands and could paint and form images like men do, they would give gods their animal images and horses would draw them as horses and oxen as oxen. Ethiopians would make their gods with dark skin and prominent nose and Thracians would depict them red-haired and blue-eyed. . . .[66]

In fact, gods are thought of as co-habiting, like humble mortals, in typical family groups. Fathers, mothers, children, siblings – it is the human family displayed in heaven. However, it is not possible to know exactly when this displacement towards celestial mansions started. The historical beginnings of religious beliefs are impossible to know for sure. It seems likely, however, that they are the product of primitive man's oneiric fantasies. In his dreams, the dreadful and ferocious archaic father first manifested himself in horrible visions. But he did it, just like in the dreams of contemporary man, through the clothing of symbol. It was not the father, but God. Thus, it was not easy for our remote ancestor, as it is not for the child, to accurately differentiate upon waking, dream from reality. Oneiric images were considered part of the real world since for man as for the immortal Segismund of Calderón de la Barca (1600–1681), frontiers between life and dream were always ambiguous: "What is life? An illusion, a shadow, a fiction. . . ."[67]

For this reason, religious myths are merely collective dreams of primitive humanity. The indelible features of those remote times are portrayed in their dramatic fabric. Gods are always driven by motives all too human.

In light of these facts, the theological statement that God is our father is psychologically justified. The belief in God has its origin in the child's first reactions towards his parents. The identity between father and god is evident. It is always present in religious language and encompasses the representative of god on earth: Papst, padre, père, Pope. Thus, the English psychoanalyst, Ernest Jones, in *The Psychology of Religion* (1926), said:

> . . . religious life represents a dramatization on a cosmic plane of emotions, fears and wishes which arose in the relation of the child with his father.[68]

This is why the character of gods varies according to the spirit of the people who unconsciously create them. Thus, as an expression of the soul of ancient Greece, the Olympic gods were full of joy and sensuality, and cruelty too; whereas the somber and despotic Jehovah of the Old Testament, is a clear manifestation of the Jewish temperament of that era. Gods, like a mirror, reveal their own people. In addition, faithful to their familial inspiration, religious systems have culminated more and more in the cult of the trinity: father, mother and son. In the Christian religion, the image of the mother has been partially eclipsed by the ghost, although in Catholic countries, the widespread cult of the Virgin Mary has elevated her to divinity as mother.

We should not be surprised then, when facing the historical development of religious beliefs, to discover that the same violence we observed in lower animals, as well as in primitive man towards his children, still survives in these sublime versions of the human family.

The archaic father shifted from the earth to heaven, but evidently took no care to shift his character during the journey. Castration and anal submission were retained in real or symbolic form, after specious theological justifications regarding the fate of "the children of god."

The case of the Christian Skoptzy sect represents an impressive example. This sect had its origin in the 18th century in Russia, and prolonged its existence until early in this century. All male members were castrated and their wives prostituted themselves with their husbands' permission in order to avoid the extinction of the group. The main prophet of the sect of the castrated was Condrati Selivanov. The *British Encyclopedia* has this to say about him:

> Selivanov was a countryman and he started his religious career as Andrei Ivanov's assistant who had been accused by the Czar's police of convincing thirteen other peasants to practice genital self-mutilation. As a result of this episode, both men were taken to prison and then sent to

> Siberia. Selivanov was able to come back and proclaimed himself as "God's son" in the flesh of Peter III, very popular emperor among the countrypeople. Later on he added the degrees of "God of Gods" and "King of Kings." He announced the divine testimony that believers who practiced voluntary self-mutilation would be saved. Through these means he was able to convince and convert noblemen, military men and even priests from other sects. He lived in Saint Petersburg for eighteen years in one of his disciples' residence, living a double homage–as Christ and as the Czar. In 1779 he was arrested, this time following the order of Paul I, and he was admitted to a hospice. Under the regime of Alexander I, he was released but in 1820 he was locked in a monastery in Szerdal, where he died in 1832 at the age of one hundred.[69]

The Skoptzy called themselves "the clean," "the fair," "the sons of the Lord." They claimed that God had created his children to live in sexual abstinence (like colts or monkeys expelled from the troop or horde). Original sin consisted, in fact, of violating this mandate of the celestial father. Therefore, it could only be expiated by removal of the sinful organs–the genitals. Once castrated, the sect members would have the door to heaven open again.[70]

The sect literally followed the teachings of Jesus in the *Gospel According to Saint Matthew*, Chapter XIX, verse 12.

> . . . for there are some eunuchs, which were so born from their mother's womb; and there are some eunuchs, which were made eunuchs of men; and there be eunuchs, which have made themselves eunuchs for the Kingdom of heaven's sake. He that is able to receive it, let him receive it.

The members of the sect often cited another exhortation of the Redeemer as well (Chapter XVIII, verses 8 and 9):

> Wherefore if thy hand or thy foot offend thee, cut them off, and cast them from thee: it is better for thee to enter into life halt or maimed, rather than having two hands or two feet to be cast into everlasting fire.
>
> And if thine eye offend thee, pluck it out, and cast it from thee: it is better for thee to enter into life with one eye, rather than having two eyes to be cast into hell fire.

Without being psychoanalysts, the Skoptzy clearly perceived the transparent genital symbolism of the limbs and the eyes and neatly submitted to the divine mandate. Two types of "purifications" or castrations were applied to those who were initiated: the "Imperial" one or "Great seal," which consisted of amputating the penis and the testes, and the "Small" one, in which only the scrotum was removed.[71]

The behavior of this sect was unique and removed from the liturgy of the great Christian churches; however, it was not nonsensical. On the contrary, its logic was strictly based on divine exhortations. Nowadays, there is no lack of substitutes for those sinister ceremonies. In analyzing the Church of Rome itself, we may ask if the Catholic priest's vow of chastity is not a symbolic castration? Moreover, the tunic adopted by the clergy has been a symbol of the ritual of self-castration in many other religions before Christianity. For instance, the priests of Astarte, the Phoenician goddess to whom human sacrifices were offered, were so dressed immediately after being mutilated.[72]

In any case, in the course of history, castration has not been the only way of ritual submission to the father of the heavens. As pointed out by Theodor Reik, in *Masochism in Modern Man* (1949), there are other ways, such as being used as a woman, raped or inseminated.[73] A remnant of this atavistic type of anal humiliation is still unconsciously manifested in the Islamic religion. The Mussulman must pray five times a day. When he prays to Allah, he prostrates himself with his head bent to the ground and his forehead towards Mecca and the Kaaba – and his ass raised in the air. The word *mussulman* derives from *muslimin*, meaning "one who surrenders," and *Islam* means "submission."[74]

X

Sexual submission to the father, masked in homosexual pleasure, was patently revealed in the psychoanalysis of one of my patients. He was a young man, aged 21, who was consumed by a stubborn erotic fantasy. It constituted his favorite fantasy during masturbation. In it, he would see himself lying naked on his stomach, and on top of him was his younger friend trying to penetrate him anally. The image was an accurate representation of a real scene that had happened a year before. In fact, his homosexual relations had not gone beyond his experiencing the pressure of his juvenile lover's cock on his anal orifice. Penetration had never taken place. Nevertheless, this sexual game sufficed to become the central piece in his erotic fantasies. He felt joyfully humiliated during the event. In addition, he experienced a special, voluptuous sensation of degradation when he remembered the malevolent and aggressive question of his mate who would ask, while pushing determinedly with his penis: "Do you like it?" And the pleasant submission reached its climax when he felt obliged to answer him, quietly, "Yes."

Joy was then almost ineffable. It was not only degrading oneself, but acknowledging it! To utter it with his own lips! To listen to his own voice! Orgasm always arrived in the middle of this subjugation. But after ejaculation, a feeling of disgust and shame overcame him. He felt incapable of looking his parents in the eye, he was prey to deep remorse, and promised himself to give up his perverse wishes forever. He would redeem himself. He would never think of this again. He would be a new man!

His determination was sincere but it only lasted until the reappearance of sexual arousal. Then, slowly at the beginning but more strongly afterwards, he let himself be seduced by the old, familiar images. Sexual heat enwrapped him, until he found himself finally paralyzed by his fantasies. And once again he was at it!

Psychoanalysis slowly revealed the hidden roots of his masochist passion. His first associations led us to puberty. He could clearly remember the awakening of his sexuality; it had surprised him with great force. He experienced a whirlwind of erotic sensations. His first desires were directed towards a blonde, beautiful, young servant, but the girl was far from eager to please him. His first adventure ended in failure, and unfortunately, it was not the only one. His virile wishes could not reach fruition by way of the vagina. In fact, only after his failed attempts with women did homosexual longings enter his mind.

The analysis of his character was revealing. He felt great rivalry with men. He was aggressive and defiant towards them, but he was also afraid of them. He could remember a series of humiliating defeats in fights for leadership with schoolmates. When a rival avoided fighting him, dissuaded by his screaming, he would feel and act triumphantly, but confronted by the least physical resistance, he was overcome by inhibition. He could not fight. Then, always the same obsessive scene repeated itself: he ended up lying on the ground, still and paralyzed, almost begging.

On one occasion, when he was 14, he was able to get on top of his opponent, kneeling over him and controlling him. He could not, however, beat him. He could only keep him on the ground. But then, suddenly the situation was reversed and his rival got on top of him. The latter showed no mercy and hit him on the head until, humiliated, he had to utter the ritual, shameful words that stopped the combat: "I give in."

After he had told me about that event during analysis, a fruitful finding took place. The young man started to realize, more and more convincingly, that the humiliating *"I give in,"* uttered in front of his mates, and the further degrading *"Do you like it?"* from his homosexual lover resounded in his soul with the same sordid harmony. He also began to realize that anal submission had been constructed on the model of physical submission; just a small step separated one from the other, and he indeed had taken it. The male, full of fear and defeated, had thus become, subtly, a woman.

He soon realized that his tendency towards homosexual submission had a longer history, reaching back to his early childhood. At that time, no doubt, he must have suffered severe intimidation, but what, and from whom? The answer was not long in coming.

One day, in the middle of a session, a memory of his childhood assailed him. In it, he saw himself being ill-treated by a man; he was also lying on the ground, totally impotent. The man was very big, though not a stranger: It was his father. Thus had a big fight ended with his admired but dreaded father. His school experiences were merely repetition of an old theme. In every schoolmate he had unconsciously seen his dreaded father. He wanted to defeat him but unfailingly he always wound up submitting himself to him, with almost photographic accuracy. The challenge, the fight, and the final submission were the endless history of a routine but painful plot.

Then, a logical but implacable conclusion came to his consciousness. If homosexual submission was the result of prior physical submission to a man, and if the unconscious model of ill treatment was imposed by his father, did not some form of anal humiliation also occur with him? Understandably, this was very painful to contemplate. However, it was necessary to face the truth. It was the only way to be cured. Therefore, he began to see, first as a dream and more clearly afterwards, that in his homosexual partner's sadistic and cold look was also the full, impassive countenance of his father who was hitting him. Both faces overlapped disturbingly. This was a shocking but decisive experience for the patient. Yet, as this vision became clearer and more certain, his homosexual passion also vanished. The wicked pleasure inexorably subsided when the true face of the man to whom he anally humiliated himself was revealed. It was not love but masochism that chained him to his lover.

XI

To have someone's ass, then, has been the obscene phrase, the "dirty" words that have occupied our attention. Undoubtedly, they are some of the most disturbing in all the family of forbidden words. They represent a cruel and sinister world and refer to one of the most severe situations that a man may endure. Now that we have a better understanding of the meaning of these words, we notice that Freud was wrong in his speculations on this subject. Among men, the desire for *having someone's ass* has not been inspired by sodomy with women. Rather it has been the other way around. Anal submission is the result of the struggle between men; that is, the struggle between rivals in their quest for women.[75] For the defeated man, it is a way of punishment and humiliation. That is why the Marquis de Sade who sees in such an impulse an exquisite male creation, is much closer to the truth than Freud. Sodomy started among men and only then was repeated with women. Nevertheless, it is neither a sign of virility nor of masculine pride, as claimed by de Sade. On the contrary, it represents a true failure, a desperate renunciation of what was called "the pleasure of being a man"[76] by the Roman emperor, Antoninus Pius (86–161). It is a radical inversion of masculinity. Perhaps it is the single case where the word inversion is properly applied. The homosexual man is not a lover but a masochist. Vulgar language has always expressed this fact. A virile man who uses and enjoys his genitals impetuously is called "a man who goes forward." The homosexual who passively offers his ass is called "an invert." It would not be easy to find a better way of expressing male inversion than through this laconic and witty spatial metaphor.

What is the reason then, from this point of view, of the anal penetration of a woman by a man? Actually, there are several. Many times it is the only available contraceptive method, but in these cases, the idea of *having someone's ass* almost vanishes due to the use of creams and lubricants to reduce the pain caused by the introduction of the cock. Thus, the feeling of submission is reduced. Furthermore, anal penetration can also occur even in a tenderly joined couple as an occasional expression of violence. Although it is sometimes denied, aggression is a common companion to love. *Odi et amo* (I hate and love) said the Latin poet Catullus (87–54 B.C.).

In addition, anal penetration of the woman can also be an expression of underlying homosexual impulses. This occurs when a man almost exclusively prefers anal intercourse. Here the woman is just a substitute for a man. This does not mean that he sees the woman more or less clearly as a man. But, interestingly, *he* is that man! He unconsciously identifies with the woman, thus revealing his own wish to submit to anal penetration. In other words, the same man who penetrates is penetrated. This peculiar homosexual splitting of personality constitutes the typical fantasy of all obsessive anal inclinations.

However, these sadistic preferences are exceptional. The robust, healthy man does not love such complications. He prefers the traditional simplicity of the vagina. It is for him the real paradise. Thus, to enjoy it represents an experience of love not cruelty. This is an intuitive but irrefutable truth. He who has experienced it knows it. Because here, more than anywhere else, *che'ntender no la puó chi no la prova* (he who has not tried it, will never be able to understand it).

XII

Through this study, we have been able to reveal the origin of the mysterious but inextricable link between sadism and anality. The atavistic sexual submission is its inexhaustible source, since *to have someone's ass* is a sexual act, but also one of sexual violence. Pleasure and aggression are merged here, and provide the model for all other ways of anal cruelty, i.e., slaps, blows, kicks.

Moreover, we have discovered that it is always the father in his animal, human, or divine form who actually or symbolically dominates, castrates, and has his son's ass. The archaic jealous and ferocious father of the primitive horde, the father who sees in his son a dangerous rival–he is the same father, the same paternal imago who always lives within ourselves.

It is true, of course, that the modern-day father no longer subdues his sons anally. Nonetheless, he still shows traces of that exaggerated violence. Even now, on occasion, he threatens and punishes his sons with no mercy, as in the case of my young patient. That is quite enough. Spontaneously, the son will take the following steps by himself. Sexual submission will take place in his fantasy. Therein physical humiliation will become erotic submission. This is a sequence as compulsive as it is inevitable. If the rivalry with the father has its origin in rivalry over the mother, all the father's violence will be experienced deep down by the son as a sexual defeat. This fatal outcome will be facilitated by the indelible tracks unconsciously left in the son's memory by the well-known and brutal history of primitive man.

Experience teaches us that we do not only try to revive our father's ill treatment with any man of authority. We also sometimes identify with him. We identify with our father, the aggressor. Then we attack our children as our father attacked us. Thus, consciously or unconsciously, we also *have his ass.* For, there is an inflexible law in psychic processes that makes a man repeat his past when he refuses to remember it.

The ancient Greeks coined a singular myth, the story of Ixion, to express this devilish compulsion to repeat. Ixion was the king of the Lapithae of Thessali, near Mount Olympus. Zeus had granted him immortality by serving him nectar and ambrosia, but Ixion tried to seduce Zeus's wife, Hera. The father of gods punished him by tying him to a wheel of fire. As he was immortal, the endless turning of the wheel became an eternal torture for him.

How can we stop the malevolent wheel that yokes us to the eternal torment of submitting and in turn forcing our children to submit? There is only one solution: to remember. When doing this, we elevate ourselves with dignity from the compulsive submission of man to the virile rebelliousness of enriching friendship. In addition, we can also redeem our children with love from the cruel destiny of ritually suffering our own violence.

To remember genuinely, it is necessary to do so with true words; words capable of movingly summoning the shadows of the past. They are, in fact, the "dirty" words. They are also the words that will lead us to our earlier and greater emotions: to childhood, its passions and its incestuous fears. For the drama of incest is always the deep source of all the hallucination-inducing, taboo words. *Grattez l'adulte et vous trouverez l'enfant*–scratch the adult and there you will find the child.

6

THE SECRET PLEASURE

"It could also be said there is a therapeutic return to masturbation. Many of you must have undergone the experience, which means a great progress, when the patient in the course of therapy, allows himself to masturbate again—though having the purpose of not remaining in this infantile stage."

SIGMUND FREUD
(Contributions to the Symposium
on Masturbation, 1912)

I

To masturbate, according to *Webster's Dictionary,* comes from the Latin, *masturbare,* and means to procure for oneself sensual joy by one's own means.[1] The name comes from the so-called "sin of Onan," and its source is the ancient biblical tradition. The patriarch Judah had married his eldest son Her to Thamar. When his firstborn died, Judah obliged his second son, Onan, to take the widow as his wife, following ancient Egyptian and Phoenician custom. Onan hated his dead brother, and the firstborn of his marriage would be named after this dead brother. To prevent that hateful possibility, he avoided conception during coitus by ejaculating on the ground. It is not known whether to this end he practiced *coitus interruptus* with his wife, or simply achieved orgasm manually, but, in any case, since then the "sin of Onan" has been a phrase applied to solitary sexual satisfaction. Hence, the term *onanism*, which means masturbation. Men, monkeys, horses, and dogs habitually fall into it. According to Voltaire, it was very common in his time among "students, pages, and young friars."[2]

Obviously, this selfish joy is not limited only to men. The oldest written description of female masturbation is credited to the French writer, Restif de la Bretonne (1734–1806). Once he watched a dark woman, young and finely built, who had been brought up in a convent, looking at a very attractive man through a window. Suddenly, the woman showed evident signs of excitement, and then:

> I went close to her and it truly seemed to me that she was uttering tender words: she had blushed. Afterwards she sighed deeply and remained quiet, stretching her stiff legs as if they hurt.[3]

In painting, it is perhaps in *The Spring* (1478), the famous picture by Sandro Botticelli (1445–1510), where feminine onanism reaches its most beautiful though symbolic representation. It depicts the beautiful Flora[4] spreading flowers over the meadow. The young woman, of artistocratic shape and refined elegance, has the lost look characteristic of those who indulge in a charming daydream as she rests her right hand over a bunch of flowers (universal symbol of the vulva), that is painted, so as to avoid any doubts, right on her own bosom.[5]

To be sure, gratification is sought not only with the genital organs; it may also be enjoyed with other parts of the body. Many masturbatory practices of homosexual men and women consist, for example, of rhythmically introducing some hard, bulky, and long object into the ass.

In Gaius Petronius' (1st century) *Satyricon,* the greatest classic of Roman pornography, and the oldest known novel, the main character provides himself with pleasure of this sort when the priestess in the temple,

> . . . fetched a leather phallus seasoned it with pepper, nettle seeds and oil, while introducing it little by little into my ass.[6]

Actually, one's entire body can be used for these exclusive pleasures and usually they go together with rich, lascivious ideas and images. All the forbidden impulses and yearnings find here a fantastic realization. Anna O., the first patient in rudimentary psychoanalysis, called this inner world her "private theatre." The performances on this mental stage are an everpresent show for the masturbator.

Certainly, vulgar language does not use such colorless words as *masturbation* or *onanism.* Those are cold terms characteristic of the jargon of science or the dictionaries. Popular slang has a typical voice, which is obviously obscene. This sensual but selfish satisfaction is called *to jerk off,* a derivative of the Middle English, *yerken* (to beat vigorously). *Jerking off* is then another of our "dirty" words.

II

Actually, masturbation is a widespread sexual practice in spite of moral condemnation. Traditionally it was thought that one did not masturbate until puberty. This is the time when the outburst of juvenile energies leads to those well-known solitary withdrawals. Psychoanalysis, however, has challenged this settled opinion. Unbiased observation of experience does not coincide with the traditional belief. Moreover, only a stubborn denial of facts could have maintained it for so long, for it is obvious that, from the time we are very young, we devote ourselves to discovering the delicious possibilities of our flesh.

Who has not seen a baby engaged in the joyful task of sucking his thumb? Or the little boy rhythmically stretching, as if it were an elastic rubber, the skin of the prepuce of his tiny penis? Or the little girl rubbing her thighs voluptuously?

How did we fail for so long to properly evaluate what was so plain to see? The answer is obvious: it was the result of moral scruples, i.e., our conscience. Conscience not only tells us what we must do but also what we must see. It not only prevents our sensual pleasure but also upsets our view. When it forces us to deny what our eyes see, it prevents us from properly evaluating our experience. It prevents us, in short, from being intelligent!

That is why the greater the prohibition to think about sexual facts, the more intellect will be damaged. Such reasoning leads to interesting consequences for the intellectual differences between sexes. What was once called "women's mental weakness"[7] derives from this harsh prohibition. It is not biology but morality that impairs intelligence.

Bertrand Russell (1872–1970), English philosopher and Nobel Prize winner, put forward this idea in *Marriage and Morals* (1929):

> . . . it cannot be denied that on average, women are more stupid than men, and I believe this is to large extent due to the fact that during youth they are more sternly forbidden to instruct themselves on sexual matters than men are.[8]

Needless to say, men do not show an undamaged intelligence either, since moral conscience generates a strong resistance to truth in all of us. Freud considered this resistance to the facts to be a temporary fit of dementia,[9] a fleeting limitation on our intellectual faculties. Typical of this was the unbelievable idiocy he observed in his patients, who put up fierce resistance at times to acknowledging one aspect or another of their sexuality. And he added *sine ira et studio* (without anger or prejudice),

> Another instance–impossible to use scientifically–would be the remarkable imbecility we are used to finding in the arguments of our opponents, even from those who are intelligent in other aspects. This is also mere resistence.[10]

Once Ernest Jones asked the great Viennese teacher which were his favorite works. Freud took two volumes off a bookshelf–*The Interpretation of Dreams* (1900) and *A Sexual Theory* (1905)–and he said: "I trust this one to be soon outdated because of its general acceptance; yet this other one will last longer." And after an easy smile he added: "My fate seems to have been to discover only what is self-evident: that children have sexual sensations, something all nannies know. . . ."[11]

There is, certainly, no doubt about it: little children are tiny *jerkers,* too.

III

The "dirty" words *jerk off* vividly shock us. Just as with other obscene words they cause us to visualize the sexual experience. As we know, this is so because the conflict between instinct and prohibition leads to a traumatic situation, which in turn calls forth its peculiar hallucinatory power. We *see* the man, the woman, or the child yielding to the secret pleasure. Also, we do feel the indefinable apprehension that arises when a taboo is violated. Moral conscience has left its deleterious print on our souls through time. Who has not heard, over and over again, admonitions from watchful parents: "Do not touch yourself!" "I will hit you on your hands!" "Stop doing that, you nasty kid!" Or warnings even more frightening: "I will cut it off."

The fierce ban on masturbation has known no boundaries in our culture. There were times when it reached truly preposterous proportions. In the Victorian era, infibulation of adolescents' prepuces, by means of a ring or some other device, to prevent onanism was suggested and widely discussed at a scientific meeting. Cages or clamps were also invented for young men's cocks (the keys to these cages were kept by fathers), and there was even an electrical device which reported any infantile erection with the ring of a bell in the parents' bedroom![12]

Jerking off thus has come to be a never-ending source of guilt and shame in our culture. It has become a secret vice and as such the offender is threatened with terrible consequences: mental retardation, brain softening, loss of teeth, weakening of the spinal cord. So indelible is the imprint of our first taboos, that these childish fears sometimes continue into adulthood, even though masturbation, of course, cannot produce these dire consequences.

Fear of a hump, for instance, a typically male anxiety, originates in these sources. The humped over position is one of the characteristic postures a man assumes when he–as Quevedo put it–decides to "live in concubinage with his own hand,"[13] i.e., seated, bending his back, and watching his cock. The abnormal protuberance would thus be both a reminder of the sin as well as a punishment.

Obviously, moral evaluations of onanism have not been quite the same over history. In the view of the Greeks, as opposed to Jewish and Christian thought, the sexual instinct was considered a divine impulse. The gods were always depicted–whether in sculpture, painting, or poetry–in the full splendor of the flesh. Sexuality was a fresh and spontaneous ingredient of everyday life in classic Greece. It was expressed in statues, paintings, vases, and terracotta lamps, even children's dishes had drawings of men and women engaged in the art of love. Statues of Priapus, protector of gardens and orchards, who had a colossal phallus, were on street corners. Single and married women kneeled in front of them begging for the gift of fertility.[14] On the eve of their wedding night young girls leaned on them and candidly offered their virginity to the god.

It is no surprise, then, to find in such a free environment, that there were shoemakers who manufactured leather phalluses for ladies wanting to masturbate.[15] In the British Museum there is a glass bearing on its surface the painting of a courtier carrying the exciting prosthesis, called an *olisbos*,[16] and in the Boston Museum of Fine Arts it is possible to see two glasses from Attica with black figures, painted by the Amasis Painter, which represent two men engaging in masturbation of their long penises.[17] Also in Aristophanes' play *Lysistrata*, onanism is immodestly exposed. The play was performed in 412 B.C. and was written to dissuade Athenian men from continuing the never-ending, disastrous Peloponnesian war against Sparta. Women decided to deprive their husbands of the joys of love until they settled the matter with the enemy. Lysistrata, their leader, stated her complaint like this:

> There is not even the shadow of a man left to commit adultery with. And, since the Milesius betrayed us I have not seen even an eight-finger-long leather phallus to console us in our widowhood. . . .[18]

In a world that worshipped the human body, joyous adventures related to it were carried out with a clean conscience. In *Les Chansons de Bilitis* (1894), a Greek courtier pays a sensual, though private, tribute to her own breasts:

> Flesh in blossom, oh, my breasts!, how rich they are in voluptuousness! In my hands, how you do show yourselves loaded with infinite sweetness and soft tender and warm perfume!
>
> Long ago you were as icy as a statue's bosom, and as hard as the insensitive marble. But since you ripened I love you still more, perhaps because you have been loved.
>
> Your generous and smooth shape is the pride of my dark torso. And whether I hold you captive within a golden

> net or show you naked, you always precede me with your splendor.
>
> Enjoy yourselves tonight. If my fingers discover new caresses, only you shall know until tomorrow; since tonight, Bilitis gives herself to Bilitis.[19]

What a different world from ours! A great gap separates us from it, but it is even greater than the 2,000 years separating us in time. It is a moral distance. Today, masturbation is so burdened with immoral connotations that it seems insulting to characterize Bilitis' joyous nocturnal surrender as such. However, it was simply *jerking off* that she engaged in during that night of lonely fondling. These harmonious lines leave us with a great lesson. We thought onanism was necessarily a tainted practice. Evidently this is not so. In fact, it appears that only our ideas about it are corrupt. Morality invalidates the innocence of our instincts. Nature is never vicious, though our prejudices may well be so. Perversion is not in *jerking off* but in our minds. As Shakespeare so eloquently put it: "Conscience does make cowards of us all" (*Hamlet*, III,1).

IV

The French philosopher Diderot denounced chastity as unnatural and approved of *jerking off* as an indispensable relief:

> Nature tolerates nothing useless. So then how can I be reproached for helping it when it asks for my assistance by means of the least ambiguous of all symptoms? We

> should never provoke it, but give it a hand now and then.[20]

Indeed, it is a great advance when the patient during therapy allows himself to practice masturbation again, though, of course, with no intent of going on forever with his hermetic pleasure. "To give nature a hand now and then" presumes a healthy progress for the patient. He must experience, without shame or fear, all his instinctive impulses. He must accept himself thoroughly so that he can become aware of the deep truth concealed in the well-known lines of the Latin playwright, Terentius (185–159 B.C.): *homo sum; humani nihil a me alienum puto* (I am a man; nothing human is alien to me). Only in this way will he be able to continue with his normal sexual growth.

V

It is true that masturbation is never a final destination. On the contrary, what is natural during childhood becomes a hindrance in time. Experience teaches us that human beings, the same as animals, *jerk off* only when they are unable to have sexual intercourse, either because of moral prohibitions or physical restraints. Onanism always blooms in places where frequent intercourse between the sexes is banned: prisons, monasteries, and military quarters, or in situations like the one described in Martial's *Epigrams* (X, 104–105):

> Phrygian slaves masturbate behind the doors, whenever Andromaca rides Hector's horse.[21]

Lovers, of course, often include masturbatory practices as part of their love making. Ovidio taught in his *Art of Love*, III, concerning Olivia, third wife to the great Roman Emperor who ". . . has never yet disdained to lend her gentle and plump hand to light up Augustus' desires."[22]

Yet these gifts are bestowed as a prologue or suggestive overture but never as a final act. This is so because if these playful practices were carried to their final stages, they would leave an aftertaste of dissatisfaction in the lovers; a feeling of incompleteness and imperfection. (The chronic masturbator, for example, lives in a permanent stage of apathy, fatigue, and bad temper.) This is so because vaginal coitus is an irreplaceable biological need. It has been so determined by the evolution of the species, and supported by the authority of time. Onanism, instead, is just a temporary haven. Even the most pleasurable *jerking off* is nothing but a poor substitute for coitus. Thus, when condemning masturbation, the prohibition has done nothing but cruelly and gratuitously complicated a pleasure already deficient in itself.

In his captivating memoir, *Fragment of a Great Confession* (1949), Reik frankly describes this painful instinctive involution. His candor is unusual among psychoanalysts, since Freud bequeathed to his disciples a legacy of extreme discretion in matters sexual. Although he once mentioned "the indiscretions I am forced to commit"[23] when editing the interpretation of some of his own dreams, he was in fact a great concealer of his own sexual life. In the various comments about himself, scattered throughout his works, he sometimes appears vengeful, mean, ambitious, or even patricidal–but never sensuous![24]

Freud's students obediently followed his example.

Indeed, if we were to believe the literature on psychoanalysis, none of them *jerked off*. Reik, in his sincerity, was a precious exception.

Reik's wife suffered from a serious heart disease. It was a chronic illness, with frequent painful periods. Reik was 34 years old at the time and had to face the painful truth that he no longer could have sexual intercourse with her. Thus, he had to choose among sexual abstinence, unfaithfulness, or masturbation. He believed that a person could not do without some form of sexual pleasure for too long; neurosis or physical disease was the unavoidable toll of such abstinence. He stated that he was fully aware that ". . . the blessing of perfect chastity was limited to the few God particularly loves: saints and people poor in spirit. In other words, to the sick ones."[25] So, he chose masturbation. With unusual openness, he relates, however, the instinctive regression that onanism meant for him:

> A thirty-five-year-old man who, owing to external and inner circumstances is forced to seek refuge in masturbation, does not usually feel guilty, and least of all in the way a nine- or ten-year-old child may. It is not necessarily so. Quite often this way of sexual pleasure may cause other negative reactions, such as shame. That is, the man feels as degrading, noxious to his esteem as a person and as a man, to have to make use again, being (already) an adult, of this infantile procedure. He experiences it as something not compatible with his age and maturity. It is as if the President of the Guaranty Trust Co. joined five- or six-year-old children for playing marbles at the corner instead of visiting golf links.[26]

VI

Freud did not believe in the value of chastity, either. On the contrary, he thought it pernicious since man's sexual behavior is the unconscious model of his way of being in the world:

> I have never had the impression that sexual abstinence had helped men of independent actions, or original thinkers, or courageous liberators, or reformers, in any way; man's sexual behaviour is frequently a symbol of his way of reacting before the outer world. A man who energetically takes the woman he desires will probably show the same zeal and tenacity when pursuing other ends.[27]

What holds true for continence holds also true for masturbation. Both set a harmful psychic prototype. Those who get used to solitary pleasures in the world of fantasy lose the will to take part in the real world, to modify it, and to make it malleable to their wishes. They become beings who think but do not act, and their lives are wasted in manipulating daydreams. Vulgar language has defined them with great psychological perspicacity. It calls them *jerks*. They are the kind of people who make passivity their style. Their lives are a record of frustrated projects and unfinished initiatives. A mysterious force inhibits them from crossing the border separating the world of ideas from the world of facts.

Obviously, they are characters not to be envied. However, to our astonishment, there are those who not only suffer from such a mediocre destiny but also praise it! They are people who have made a virtue out of necessity. They have sometimes even justified their secret pleasures through philosophical arguments. Indeed, it is common practice to devise philosophical doctrines to support unconscious tendencies. Moreover, such is the true source of philosophical creativity for many people. Thus,

Nietzsche in "Beyond Good and Evil" (1885) taught that all philosophers are "lawyers who refuse to be so called, and in most cases they are naughty sponsors of their own prejudices, which they baptize as 'truths.'"[29]

Such is the case, for example, with the Greek philosopher Aristotle (384–322 B.C.). Some people believe that the spiritual history of the West is inconceivable without him. Dante, in his great poem, said Aristotle's philosophy was that of *di coloro che sanno* (the ones who know). Centuries, then, have bestowed upon him the honorary title of *Ille Philosophus* (The Philosopher).

Aristotle loved the contemplative life. It was the sole truly human life for him. In his work, *Nichomachean Ethics* (I, 1904–5–8), he asks, "What is the supreme good?" Happiness, undoubtedly, but when he inquires as to what happiness is, he admits the answer is not at all clear. Ordinary people and sages do not agree on the matter. However, so the grave philosopher argues, it has to be located in an activity exclusive to man, something that sets him apart from animals and plants. And what characterizes the human being is the use of the mind in accordance with reason. For Aristotle, then, happiness can be found in the intellectual life. Such was the reasoning of our illustrious philosopher!

Indeed, one of the most precious merits of intellect is that since it is merely contemplative, it has no goal beyond itself. It is self-sufficient and derives pleasure from itself. Hence, Aristotle claims in his *Politics* (1267a):

> Those who long for an independent joy must search for it in Philosophy, since all other pleasures require the assistance of other human beings.[29]

Aristotle coined an image of a god that also fit his notions of the happy man. It is a god who never does anything, a god who has neither wishes nor will. His only activity is to contemplate the essence of things, and since he himself is the essence of everything, his only task consists of contemplating himself. In his *Metaphysics* (XII, 7, 1074–5) Aristotle says that god:

> Thinks of himself, since he is the optimum, and his thought is a thought of thoughts. . . . And there he is being an act of thought which thinks itself over during the whole eternity.[30]

He is a lazy god to whom the "sweetest and most excellent activity is contemplation. . . ."[31] He is a *roi fainéant* (an idle king) and a great loner. Unlike the divine Jupiter's sensual dissipations and heavenly couplings, the activities of this god are foreign to the Greek soul. It has fairly been said that he seems a copy of Aristotle himself. The latter loved contemplation so much he sacrificed the image of the deity to it. Yet to define god as an inactive being "who thinks himself over during the whole eternity" is a way of characterizing, elliptically, a masturbator. Thus the Aristotelian god is disclosed to us, suddenly and irreverently, as a *jerking-off* god!

Moreover, since this god is but a creature of his creator, he reveals with his effigy, interesting and hidden aspects of the immortal philosopher's erotic life. Such knowledge becomes a reward that greatly satisfies our psychological curiosity, since finding out some of the relationships between philosophers' personalities and their works was, for Freud, one of the ways in which, "Philosophy might receive the impulse of psychoanalysis, that is, becoming its object."[32]

VII

A young patient helps shed further light on our subject. He was 24 years old, single, and a university student. He was dating a nurse one year older than himself. She was a tall, thin woman, dark skinned, and her face had particularly delicate features. His sex life was, however, very limited. He could feel almost no pleasure in vaginal coitus. Instead, he would rather suck the girl's large breasts while she tenderly helped him jerk off.

Inasmuch as their meetings were sporadic, in the intervals he often used to masturbate while thinking of her. He had one fantasy that particularly excited him. He imagined the young woman leading him to the restroom, then holding his cock and making him piss. He so much enjoyed this fantasy that finally, one day, he wanted to experience it in reality. His lover was surprised and the suggestion made her blush. Nonetheless, he convinced her to try it, and so they went to the restroom. There, the girl gingerly unbuttoned his fly, and held his stiff, almost violet cock in her hand. Then slowly, piss started to flow like a fountain.

The young man experienced a strong upsetting feeling as he related this adventure during therapy. He did not hesitate in stating that what he had done was a degrading and morbid act.

On another day, during a session in which he was talking about his baffling urinary experience, an unexpected memory cropped up. He saw himself as a little boy, just five, with his mother, in the toilet. She was looking at him, smiling motheringly, while she held his *little dick,* which was hard, to help him pee.

It was then that he had a sudden intuition. Was it not

possible that his wicked wish was merely a longing to repeat what had happened with his mother? He thought it extraordinary, unbelievable, and yet, at the same time, a feeling of certainty was quickly growing in him. The scene that aroused so much voluptuousness in him turned out to be the repetition of an innocent childhood experience. However, substitution of characters had taken place. It was no longer him as a child but as an adult, and the lady was not his mother but a nurse. Besides, there was another great difference. During childhood he had always experienced a candid sensual pleasure when his mother held his little penis between her fingers. It was an intimate pleasure that he enjoyed in full consciousness. It is natural that a mother should teach her child to piss! But at present when this childhood wish turned up again, masked, it came together with oppressive guilt, and an unnerving feeling of wickedness.

What had happened? The answer is plain. Between the child's satisfaction and the adult's reproduction of that satisfaction, moral conscience intervenes. And thus ends the carefree and happy period of "infantile immorality."[33] From then on remorse and shame are the toll for pleasure. This is an inexorable, universal process. Somehow, every child knows that the periodic and delicious meeting of his tiny penis with his gentle mother's hand will end. Too many signs warn him. And he has to endure, without understanding, how what used to be so good yesterday has become wicked today.

The story should not only teach us but also stimulate some profitable thoughts. Above all, we have realized, that it is the mother who teaches the child to discover the huge range of pleasurable possibilities of his own body. When she holds his tiny cock, she leaves an indelible imprint on his soul; one he will later follow with his own hand. All her caresses, all the baths and the perfumes, disclose for her son his own skin and its delights. Such and no other is the trace left by breast-feeding as well. For, indeed, what is the pleasure of masturbating while sucking one's thumb, if not the repetition of the ineffable pleasure of sucking one's mother's tit?

Undoubtedly, our mother is our first teacher on *jerking off.* With her kind teaching, as Freud pointed out, she merely fulfills a duty imposed upon her by nature. She teaches her child to discover his own body and its amorous possibilities.[34] What is more, she offers herself, unconsciously, as an inspiring image for his solitary caresses. Openly, or covered by the loincloth of symbol–as in the case of our youthful patient's nurse–she forever occupies a privileged place in her son's private theater.

VIII

Hence do we realize that by analyzing the ban on using the "dirty" word *jerk off*, we again arrive at that familiar place; that same source, feeding the prohibition against all "dirty" words. Namely, it is the fear of incestuous thoughts and feelings. The "dirty" word, used with a genuine drive, threatens to re-awaken disturbing memories. It is therefore necessary to hush such insinuating voices.

Moral conscience is so implacable because the will to forget is so strong. Moral conscience wants to cause a gap in time: to break the historic continuity between the child and the man. It seeks to blanket childhood with amnesia. Psychoanalysis, on the other hand, aims at exactly the opposite. It aims at remembering, and since words are its only tools, it favors the most moving ones; which means, of course, "dirty" words. It is aware that they will help re-awaken the past. Such is the only road to sanity. In fact, in order to attain mental integrity, it is necessary to recover the child living within every man. For, as the English poet Wordsworth (1770–1850) said, perhaps anticipating Freud's findings, the child is the father of the man, and a natural piety should link them together all the days of his life.

7

THE SUPREME PROHIBITION

"He watched the beautiful curving drop of her haunches. That fascinated him today. How it sloped with a rich down-slope to the heavy roundness of her buttocks! And, in between, folded in the secret warmth, the secret entrances!"

D. H. LAWRENCE
(Lady Chatterley's Lover, Chapter XV, 1928)

I

We have analyzed so far a series of "dirty" words: *tits, suck tit, suck cock, shit, piss, have the ass, jerk off,* and we have discovered the need for denying some aspects of our human nature because of the prohibitions against using these terms. We have not yet discussed the supreme prohibition. We have not reached the most severely forbidden domain, that is, the ineffable experience of coitus – where moral interdiction reaches its highest point.

The dirtiest of the dirty words are: *fuck, cock,* and most of all, *cunt.* These are the words definitely expelled from any educated dialogue. They are, of course, excluded from any decent dictionary, and it would be unimaginable to hear them issue from the lips of a teacher in any classroom. A decidedly hallucinatory effect is provoked when hearing these words. They represent the favorite ingredient in off-color jokes because the purpose of every smutty joke is to surprise by calling forth the vivid representation of a sexual organ or relationship. Every joke relies on surprise. That is why we do not laugh at old jokes. Although jokes do not reveal their secret frankly, they do so indirectly. The period of time that separates the end of the story and the outburst of laughter marks the process by which, unconsciously, we catch the meaning of the allusion – which is always a sexual show. Thus, for example, this academic joke:

> A well-known professor at a university, who used to flavor his poorly amusing discipline with numerous jokes, was once congratulated on the birth of a new son born when the professor was quite of age. "Thank you, thank you," he replied, "you can see what wonders a man's hand is capable of doing."[1]

Or this *lapsus linguae,* true and funny:

> While talking in a meeting about a topic which, according to the enthusiasm of her words, seemed to cause in her secret emotions, a lady said the following: "Yes, a woman needs to be beautiful to appeal to men. Men have less difficulty in attracting women. Provided he has five members very straight."[2]

The image of the *cock* in both cases is reproduced before our eyes. That and no other was, of course, the purpose of the witty remarks. That is also the reason why obscene jokes are mainly told by men in the presence of women. It involves an attempt of aggressively displaying before them one's manhood. It is, therefore, a type of sexual pass. But it is also a deliciously virile attack. Women do not tell off-color jokes!

In a subtle and captivating aesthetic study, Freud accurately pointed out this peculiar hallucinatory character of "dirty" words:

> The off-color saying is like undressing the person of the other sex to whom it is directed with its obscene words, it obliges the attacked person to fancy the part of the body or action to which they correspond making her see that the attacker is now showing them. Undoubtedly, the pleasures of watching sexual parts totally unveiled is the primary motive of this type of saying.[3]

The off-color joke is always a way to overcome prohibition. We say humorously what we cannot say seriously. It is a step forward, yet, it presupposes the interdiction. It does not defeat it; it just avoids it. Among people of more relaxed morality, sexual boldness need not be humorous to be expressed. It is spontaneous and frank, it has no veils. Thus, laughter in relation to erotic matters is always ambiguous. It does not necessarily mean happiness. It is often just a momentary escape from oppression. Deep and free sexuality is removed from laughter. Love can sometimes be playful, but voluptuousness is something serious. The German philosopher, Schopenhauer (1788–1860), said that the powers of Nature work seriously everywhere.[4] Laughter in connection to sexual matters, contrary to what is popularly believed, is not so much evidence of freedom, but of censorship. It is worth remembering here the phrase of an Oriental philosopher who, after visiting a foreign country, said with simplicity and accuracy: "These people laugh a lot, they are not happy."

II

What a great emotional distance there is between the terms *fuck* and *coitus* or between *cock* and *penis* or, most of all, between *cunt* and *vagina* or *vulva.* "Dirty" words have a strange spell. They magically reproduce before our eyes, the organ or the corresponding sexual relationship. Not all "dirty" words have the same power. Magic exists in direct proportion to prohibition. The more condemned the word, the greater is its hallucinatory power. (Moral prohibition provokes the effect of a trauma, of a bomb explosion. It is, besides, a foreign body encrusted in the soul.) Thus, the different power of taboo words gives rise to a scale of values among them; a scale that we cannot verify with any instrument but that we intuitively sense. Thus, we intuitively recognize that to say *fuck* is morally serious but to say *cock* is worse, and even more so, *cunt*!

But, why? That there is a hierarchy among "dirty" words is certain, but the order of the series is still rather strange. Since coitus is the most pleasurable experience provided by nature to humans and since sexuality is the favorite terrain of moral conscience, *fuck* ought to be the most banned word. Nevertheless, experience indicates that this is not so. *Cock* and *cunt* claim the dubious honors.

In light of these facts, an obvious question arises. Is it possible that sexual organs are more prohibited than sexual intercourse? We can answer affirmatively without hesitation. This is due to their strange hallucinatory power. The terms *cock* and *cunt* reproduce with great accuracy and visual impact the corresponding organs. We *see* them with all their charm and splendor: their shape, size, color, and sometimes even their odor. The word *fuck,* instead, does not cause us to visualize the sexual organs in the same way. On the contrary, it rather conceals them. True, it calls up an image of a couple during coitus, but their genitals are mingled and cannot be seen! (This is the reason why photographs of coitus in pornographic magazines, in their effort to show the penis and vagina in any way, are usually far-fetched.) It is clear that in the moment of penetration, genitals disappear and we see only the bodies of the lovers melted in their amorous embrace. This is why the word *fuck* is relatively less condemned.

Discoveries made in the excavations of Pompeii fortunately provide us with a wonderful opportunity to verify our intuition. The Roman city had been founded by the Oscans, one of the ancient peoples of central Italy on the Mediterranean coast, near Naples at the foot of the Vesuvius volcano. It was buried by lava in the year 79 B.C. Excavations started in 1748 and continued until our century. Thus, very valuable testimony of its inhabitants' lives and art have come to us: temples, official and private buildings, streets, theaters, and even a brothel! This whorehouse constitutes an archeological treasure of incomparable value since it provides much data on the sexual habits of that time. The numerous frescos discovered in its ruins illustrating the voluptuous specialties of the house represent an insurpassable *racconto,* a magnificent exhibition of ancient sexuality. Representations of coitus, as sung by Ovidio (43 B.C.–17 A.D.), show women in the most varied lustful positions: "et faciunt cura ne videantur anus; utque velis Venerem iungunt permille figuras; invenit plures nella tabella modos"[5] ("mature women surrender to love in thousands of positions which cannot be found in any list of lascivious paintings; voluptuousness is provoked in them without contrivances").

What is especially interesting for us is that none of the Pompeian paintings of coitus show both sexual organs openly observed. Sometimes the penis is evident, but the vulva never appears in the foreground. At most, we can observe its hair. This is very significant in understanding the hierarchy among dirty words. It allows us to estimate the existent values, since it is not difficult to suspect that the least shown is the most prohibited. The cunt is thus, by exclusion, the most condemned vision.

The *Raccolta Pornográfica* verifies our observations. It is the collection of obscene objects rescued from Pompeii. It was referred to as such by Alexandre Dumas, *père* (1801–1870), in 1860, when he happened to be director of the museum of Naples. That is the name it still retains, and it represents an invaluable item of our cultural heritage. Among its more than 200 pieces and objects of art, there are innumerable phallic reproductions: carvings, statues, frescos, fountains, tripods, sculptures, glasses, sarcophagi, mirrors, plates, amphoras, and lamps. In this unusual pornographic collection, the male member is shown in its varied shapes, sizes, and colors. Yet, there is not one vulva! The vulva stands out by its absence. Evidently, a supreme prohibition was placed upon it; what must not be seen, was not seen. Not even in a brothel! All of which leads us to conclude: The cunt is the most banned image, and the dirtiest of the "dirty" words.

III

As a matter of fact, if we conducted a random survey among men, asking them for an accurate description of the vulva–its shape, size, and color–we would have a puzzling result: they are not able to do so.

Only then would they notice with surprise that they hardly look at it when making love. They hardly ever stop to observe the details of the "secret entrance." Even those who enjoy *lambendo lingua genitalia* (licking the genitals) would realize that they do not study it thoroughly. A man who has no difficulty in recalling the smallest features of a drawing, or the slightest lines of a statue, or the most delicate typographies of a book, will not be able, however, to describe the vulva accurately! It would be difficult to find a territory so much ignored by men as the geography of the *cunt.* This great paradox, then, is the consequence of moral prohibition. A disorientation takes place via the influence of moral scruples, such that the most desired becomes the most feared. Horror takes the place of love.

So it happened, for instance, in the ancient Greek world. It has left us, symbolically in its myths, a terrifying image of the female genital: Medusa's face. She was one of the mythic Gorgons, the sisters who inhabited the far west of the Earth in the proximity of Hell. They had a monstrous appearance: enormous head and serpent-like hair, long sharp teeth, bronze hands, and golden wings. Their eyes scintillated, and one who dared look at them became petrified. Of the three sisters only Medusa was mortal. She was so dreadful that she not only frightened men but gods as well. Perseus, Zeus's son, by using a shield polished like a mirror, through which he looked at the monster indirectly, cut off her head while she was asleep.

Freud, who seldom interpreted individual mythological subjects, could not resist in the case of the decapitated head of Medusa. He did not hesitate to invoke here an equation which subsequent psychoanalytic work has shown to be valid, namely, that beheading is a symbol of castration.[6]

Castration is a punishment. It is the punishment a child will receive if he tries to enjoy his mother sexually. After the analysis of countless patients and thousands of dreams,[7] this was one of the great discoveries that Freud bequeathed to the world. Thus, referring to another Greek tragedy, he made this notion famous under the name of the "Oedipus complex."

Oedipus, who killed his father Laius, later unknowingly married his mother Jocasta and had children with her. When he realized what he had done, he punished himself by pulling out his own eyes, thus symbolizing castration of his testicles. The fear of the Medusa is then, for Freud, "a terror of castration related to the sight of something."[8] That something is, as psychoanalytic experience shows, the sight of the female genital surrounded by hair, or, more specifically, the sight of the genital of the woman whom the little child loves and most intimately knows–his mother.

The interpretation is even more detailed. Various artists, such as the Italian painter, Michelangelo Caravaggio (1573–1609), in his painting of a shield with the threatening face of Medusa,[9] or the Italian sculptor, Benvenuto Cellini, in his famous sculpture, *Perseus* (1554),[10] used to represent the hair of the monster with the shapes of snakes. These snakes, in spite of being horrible, are universal symbols of the penis, and thus serve to mitigate the horror of castration by standing in place for the penis. To become petrified, adds Freud, indeed means to stay hard; as hard as the penis gets when it is erect. Petrification is hence, another way of denying castration. This is the reason why Pallas Athena, the virgin goddess of Olympus, carries this awful symbol on her clothes. She becomes the unapproachable woman who repels every sexual drive, "since she shows the terrifying genitals of the mother."[11] Finally it is not any vulva but precisely the mother's *cunt* that frightens and inhibits the man.

The robust and jocund Pantagruel of *Gargantua and Pantagruel* by François Rabelais (1490?–1553), one of the authors who most enriched the French language, offers us a surprising and unsuspected confirmation of Freud's opinion on castration. The mischievous Panurgo, pleasant and frank, suggests to Pantagruel a new and inexpensive way of fortifying the walls of Paris. As he had noticed that the vulvas of the local ladies were worth less than stones, he thought they could be used as the raw material for a wall; starting at the base with the largest vulvas, then the middle-sized ones, and on top the small ones. In relation to his idea, Panurgo tells a curious story.

In the time when beasts could speak, a poor lion was walking through the woods of Bieure. All of a sudden he saw an old woman who was looking for dry sticks. When the woman saw the lion she fell down on her back in such a way that her skirt was drawn up. The lion ran up to see if the woman had hurt herself, and upon seeing her genitals he exclaimed:

> –Poor woman! Who has injured you so?–while saying this, he saw a fox far away and called him–Fellow fox, come along. I need you!
>
> When the fox came near, the lion spoke to him like this:
>
> –My friend, the good woman has been despicably wounded between her legs, the wound is big and evidently continuous, from the ass to the navel, it measures four, rather five palms; it is a terrible ax blow and I have no doubts it is an old wound. . . .[12]

Panurgo's tale comes from the 16th century. It is evident, then, that the fear of castration knows no frontiers in time or space. It could not be otherwise. Anguish springs up eternally from the great incestuous conflict that every child must bear. Rabelais's fantasy has deep roots and is universal. Moreover, the consequences are clear. If the vulva is a wound, then it means that the mother and, therefore, all women are castrated men in the eyes of their sons, those who have been savagely punished for their incestuous desires. This is the ultimate explanation of the terror. The fear of women that consciously or unconsciously, harasses so many men, is no less than fear of the *cunt,* Medusa's face, the image of castration itself.

IV

Fortunately, however, not all men have such a fantastic idea of female genitals. This is only the malignant fruit of fear. Love sees through other eyes. He who has enjoyed the sweet ecstasy that this charming hole can render, will not make such a mistake. Venus' garden, far from being the frightening place that perverse moral conscience suggests, is in fact a warm, humid, cozy resort full of delights.

The origin of the word *cunt* is quite interesting. Its etymology is shared by the French *con,* the Italian *conno,* the Portuguese *cono,* the Catalan *cony,* the Galician *cona* and the Spanish *coño*–all derived from the Latin *cunnus.*[13] The enchantment that the cunt provides is as old as its name. Poets have devoted inspired verses to it at all times. The French Ronsard (1524–1585) saw in it, with a certain confusion, "*la vermeillette fente*"[14] (a vermilion slash). His friend, Remy Belleau (1528–1577), described it as "un petit mont feutré de mousse délicate tracé sur le milieu d'un fillet escarlatte"[15] (a little mount covered by delicate moss, traced over the middle of a scarlet thread). And in our days, the Chilean Nobel prize winner, Pablo Neruda (1904–1973), exclaimed: "Oh what a giant moss! And a crater, a rose of humid fire!"[16]

No less were the tributes rendered by novelists. Thus, for instance, Pierre Louÿs, an admirer of the voluptuousness of the ancient world, has left for us a captivating description of the vulva and the vagina in his *Aphrodite (Moeurs antiques)* (1896), a vivid tale of historic Alexandria.

Djala, the Hindu slave, sings amorous melodies from her native land to Chrisis, the beautiful courtier. The melodies deliciously praise the various sensual parts of the body, and then, finally:

> Silence was made. The slave raised her hands and bent over: The courtier went on:
>
> –*It* is like a purple flower, full of honey and perfume.
>
> –*It* is like a sea Hydra, soft and alive, opened during the night.

> –*It* is the humid cave, the ever warm shelter, the asylum where man rests on his way to death.[17]

This description of the female genital is beautiful. However, it is also compromised. The idea of death appears associated to it, indicating the existence of an obsessive and unconscious link between the greatest happiness granted to man and the most disquieting omen. Also, the licentious courtier, the owner of all pleasures, is herself subjected to the archaic taboo of words, and cannot name the *cunt*! She can only use the pronoun, IT.

V

This fear of the *cunt* has had serious consequences for man beyond the obvious sexual problems it has wrought. Among other things, for example, it has altered his idea of beauty itself.

Reflection on beauty has had a long lineage. The Greek philosophers, Socrates and Hippias, provided some initial observations.[18] But the problem was not accurately formulated until the work of German philosopher Immanuel Kant (1724–1804), in his *Critique of Judgment* (1790).

There is, for Kant, a remarkable difference between the delight of the senses and aesthetic pleasure. The former is operative and the latter, instead, is contemplative. Contemplative pleasure is a spiritual pleasure exclusive to man. Operative pleasure, the enjoyment provided by using things, is on the contrary, a sensitive delight characteristic to all animals and it consists in the mere satisfaction of physiological needs. Thus, Kant believed, we only attribute beauty to an object whose contemplation causes a disinterested pleasure in us, that is to say, a pleasure free from all physiological desire. This is the satisfaction we get when for example observing a mountain, a tree, or a flower. Beauty is, in sum, an end in itself.[19]

Schopenhauer, who was largely influenced by Kant's theory, further states in his great work, *The World as Will and Idea* (1818), that the aesthetic pleasure provided by beautiful objects consists:

> for the most part, in the fact that we sink into the state of pure contemplation, freed at this interval from all will, that is, from all wish and concern; we get rid of ourselves and our intelligence stops being at the service of our will. . . .[20]

For these philosophers beauty is, then, an exquisitely contemplative pleasure which grants us enjoyment free from all selfish interest, a high spiritual value far from the stingy contingencies of the flesh. Indeed, this is the most widespread aesthetic theory based on the tremendous authority of its progenitors.

Beauty as an independent pleasure from every personal desire–is that possible? Can we imagine that aesthetic pleasure like any other pleasure, might be indifferent to sexual instinct? Experience, in a loud voice, says it is very unlikely, even impossible. Do we know of anything more interesting and practical than sexual desire?

It is possible to observe that for every robust man without major complications, there is, deep down, no other criterion for beauty than a woman. As a result, all beautiful objects are unconsciously or consciously associated with the female. For him, as for most animals–as Darwin teaches–the taste for beauty encompasses, as best as we can understand, attraction toward the opposite sex.[21] This is, undoubtedly, a much more reasonable conceptualization, one much more related to our feelings.

We constantly feel in our everyday life, with the certitude provided by deep emotion, that beauty is fed by desire. Something is beautiful because we love it, or what is the same, everything we love is beautiful. What is beautiful for us is always what we long for or desire.

It follows, then, that since woman is the natural object of sexual desire for a man, the wish to copulate is the spring of all beauty. This becomes immediately evident if we notice that nature itself only enchants us with its beauty when somehow it stirs within us reminiscences of a woman. After all, do we not often speak of "Mother" nature?

The French Nobel prize winner Anatole France (1844–1924), in one of his literary masterpieces, *Thaïs* (1890), exposed this truth. The book describes a battle between the voluptuous Thaïs, prostitute from Alexandria and Paphnutius, and a serious and austere monk who wants to convert her. But in his arduous enterprise, the monk becomes involved in a ferocious spiritual conflict. He starts feeling in his flesh the same things he condemns in the dissolute woman. Finally, he falls in love with her and tries to possess her. Then, Thaïs shows up in a vision. Conscious of being, as a woman, the principle of all beauty, she tells him:

> I am women's beauty; where are you planning to take refuge, stupid crazy man, escaping from me? You will

> find me similar to the splendor of flowers, to the flexibility of palm trees, to the flight of doves, to the frolic of gazelles, to the waves in the water, to the soft light of the Moon. . . .[22]

Thus, we have arrived at a theory very different from that stated by Kant and Schopenhauer. Beauty is not, undisputedly, disinterested pleasure. On the contrary, it is love that engenders it. Beauty is beautiful because it represents the woman or awakens reminiscences of her.

This statement is undoubtedly much more true to experience. Yet, it does not totally satisfy us either. We feel there are still some mysteries to solve. There is something not yet shown. The enigma of beauty still conceals its last secret. Let us try to get to it.

Women have always been, indeed, the inspiring muse in men's search for beauty. In the arts, the female body has always been a source of inspiration. Sometimes fatness was fashionable, like the plump women of the Flemish painter, Rubens (1577–1640); or in the amply endowed ladies of the Frenchman, Ingres (1780–1867). At other times, taste was inclined towards the almost flat-chested ladies of the Englishman, Gainsborough (1727–1788); or the slim and elongated ones of the Frenchman, Chassériau (1819–1856). There is in all this homage to the female image a singular fact, one that constitutes a valuable clue in our search for the ultimate meaning of beauty. In all this sensual art gallery, a rigorous constant takes place: the *cunt* is never drawn, or painted, or sculpted! The final target of desire never gets represented. Now, this is a very suggestive fact. But it is also explainable. It seems that it is not possible to look in a contemplative attitude–as the old philosophers suggested–at a vulva lustfully open before our eyes. No, we do not want to contemplate at all–we want to act!

This fact provides an unsuspected revelation that allows us to deepen our understanding of the aesthetic phenomenon. We can go one step further and make a much more committed suggestion. We have already seen that the woman is for man, consciously or unconsciously, the model of all beauty. If we accept that before the vulva we cannot adopt a merely contemplative attitude, does it not follow that aesthetic appreciation of the female body is based on the prohibition of looking at the vulva? Or going even further, is not the feeling of beauty the result of sexual repression? Which leads us to conclude: We have pleasure by looking because we do not allow ourselves to have pleasure by acting.

This would seem to be the ultimate explanation of aesthetic experience. To maintain the artifice that any aesthetic pleasure presupposes, it is necessary to rely on a painful fiction. It is necessary to eliminate the vulva from sight. Its very presence would call forth desire, and contemplation would give way to action. It is very difficult to remain impassive before such a stimulus. Desire would take us from vision to act. Pornographic works are based precisely on this elementary psychological principle. It is not aesthetic pleasure but lust that they seek, and consequently, the *cunt* is shown with no inhibition. There is no other aphrodisiac more powerful and effective than this.

Only by concealing "the purple flower, full of honey and perfume" from our eyes, can we get enough distance so as to resign ourselves to contemplation. That is why we call the female beautiful and worth contemplating only when she is expurgated of her genitals. However, it is evident that a female body without a vulva is a mutilated body; a true corruption of nature. Nevertheless, it is in this distorted anatomy where the feeling of beauty flourishes! Beauty is born, thus, on noxious land. It is a weird flower. Its smell is not inhaled without danger since a subtle corruption adheres to it. If it is not a flower blooming from satisfied desire but from frustrated instinct, is it not possible that the aesthetic feeling is a sick flower in spite of the prestige and philosophical praise heaped upon it? May it not also be one of the *fleurs du mal* (flowers of evil)?

The truth is that in the arts, the female body has always been isolated from genitality. Beauty and the vulva have always been excluded from one another. Moral prohibition, over the centuries, has given rise to a new and tricky erotic emotion: the aesthetic pleasure, or what is the same, a pleasure in which instinct perverts its aims. The woman is not sought for enjoyment, but for contemplation. Beauty then, becomes the alienation of desire. Freud must have had a similar idea in mind when he stated:

> It is remarkable that genital organs themselves are never considered as beautiful, in spite of the invariable exciting effect of their contemplation; instead, such a property seems to be inherent in certain secondary sexual characteristics.[23]

VI

One of the most impressive examples of this kind of sensual deviation can be found in the work of the celebrated poet, Dante Alighieri. He was, together with Beatrice, the protagonist in one of the most famous love stories. It all began when they were about nine and met at a party given by the girl's father. From then on, the puerile passion led the boy to look for all the possible occasions when he might catch a glimpse of the little girl, although it was just to watch her without being noticed.[24]

Later on, he lost sight of her until they were both 18 years old. Then, one day, the girl appeared before his eyes dressed in pure white, escorted by two gentle ladies in the street. She turned to gaze at the timid and confused Dante. That look brought him to the height of ecstasy! And so he remained, completely enraptured.[25]

In the following years, every time she turned up somewhere, the mere hope of a simple gesture from her, transformed him. He felt enwrapped in feelings of goodness and charity, such that no man was his enemy anymore. The girl looked so affable that she aroused in those who looked at her, the poet tells us, a delicious calm. "This is not a woman but one of the beautiful angels of heaven. . . ."[26]

Finally Beatrice married a member of a wealthy bank firm, and a year later she died. During his entire life, Dante had not even touched her hand or exchanged a word with her. The *grandissimo* poet, however, was not disheartened before the sovereign mandate of death. Thus, in his *Divina Commedia,* he eagerly looked for her during a wonderful trip through *Hell* and *Purgatory,* until he found her, still enchanting, in *Heaven.*

There, she smiles at him, and again she deeply moves him. Then she asks him, *"Perché la faccia mía sí t'innamora?"*[27] *("Why does my face inspire love in you?").* It was an extraordinary fact. This man who had dared walk the road that no man had before him, when finding the woman of his dreams, could only look her in the face!

The truth is that for Dante, his beloved's body started and ended in her face. So he naively says, before the vision with which he ends the *Paradiso*:

> Dal primo giorno ch'i vidi il suo viso in questa vita, infino a questa vista, non m'e il seguire al mio cantar preciso.[28]
>
> (Since the very first day I saw your face until this vision, the thread of my song was never cut.)

A beautiful face—all the anatomy of the adored woman was just that. For the immortal Dante, Beatrice undoubtedly had no *cunt.*

VII

It is evident that this was a strange passion. Dante's sexual instinct was disturbed, and the face of the beloved woman occupied in his mind the place that should naturally be taken by another "face," more distant and sensual. A subtle displacement of desire had taken place in his soul.

But, this is not an isolated example. Experience shows us, on the contrary, that we form in our minds, unconsciously, a psychic identity between the vulva and the face. Have we not already spoken of Medusa's face? This is a widespread fantasy. Even the cold anatomists, when describing the vulva, have discovered in it *labia majora* and *labia minora.* The writer, Henry Miller, says that "there are *cunts* which laugh and *cunts* which speak,"[29] and the Frenchman, Pierre de Bourdeilles (1540–1614), in his *Gallant Ladies,* insists on the same image when speaking to us of a lady who had between her legs,

> the three beautiful colors which are red, black, and white, since her lip below was red and vermilion like coral, the hair surrounding it gracefully curly and black like ebony as it should be, since it is one of her beauties, and the skin, white as alabaster, was shadowed by that black hair.[30]

Men, who do not allow themselves to enjoy the vulva of the desired woman, unconsciously transfer their feverish longings to those areas of the female body authorized by conscience. We frequently displace our desire from the vulva to the face. At the same time, the wish to copulate gives way to contemplative pleasures. This process constitutes the main reason for preoccupation with facial beauty.

The unconscious identification between the face and the female genital also gives rise to the mocking question sometimes directed to youngsters not yet initiated in sexual matters: "Tell me, do you know God's face?" Do we not sense in this nasty jest, perhaps, an explanation of the taboo that forbids primitive men from pronouncing the name of God? Perhaps the primordial effigy of divinity was the image of a vulva, and not that of a man. The *cunt* is the most authentic face of a woman.

VIII

Lady Chatterley asked her lover:

> –What is *cunt*?
>
> –An' doesn't ter know? Cunt! It's the down theer; an' what I get when I'm i'side thee; it's a'as it is, all on't.
>
> –All on't, she teased. Cunt! It's like fuck then.

> –Nay, nay! Fuck's only what you do. Animals fuck. But cunt's a lot more than that. It's thee, dost see?[31]

The vulva is a person in itself. Only through it, can a woman truly reveal herself. Man has always felt this way; he has even baptized the vulva with proper names. Lady Chatterley's became famous worldwide as Lady Jane.

Nevertheless, as we know, moral awareness has the power of turning the most attractive face into the most repulsive. The taboo of incest frequently alters the captivating face of Venus into the horrid face of Medusa.

Furthermore, the prohibition against using "dirty" words is nowhere greater than it is here. *Cunt* is the supreme "dirty" word. We experience before this proscribed term the same disturbance suffered by the inhabitants of primitive societies in front of taboo words: the same anxiety that restrains the Tolampos from the island of Célebes, the Indians from central Australia, the Indians from the Isle of Nias and the Kaffirs of South Africa.[32]

It is quite understandable. Prohibition confronts in this case the deepest and most universal incestuous desire. The vulva is always, as Freud taught, the mother's vulva; the orifice through which we have all passed, the source of an imperishable though unconscious nostalgia. There is nothing in the world more precious for a man than his mother's genitals. Besides, they are the unconscious model for all the vulvas he will later seek. For this reason, the "dirty" word *cunt* is the most taboo of all obscene words. It is in our heart of hearts, our mother's cunt. And we should never think of it!

8

THE LONGING FOR THE SEA

". . . the purpose, besides the sexual act, can be no other but can attempt by the ego—an inaccurate and awkward attempt at first, then more consciously intended, and at last partly successful—of coming back to one's mother's womb, where there is no such painful disharmony between the ego and the environment as characterized by life in the outward world."

SANDOR FERENCZI
(*Thalassa, A Theory on Genitalia, II, 1923*)

I

Replied Zeus, the cloud-gatherer:

–Hera! We can go there later. Let us lie down and enjoy love. Never has passion for a goddess or a woman spread so wide in my chest or been so overwhelming as now: I have never loved like this before![1]

With those words, the Greek poet Homer tells us in the *Iliad* (XIV), the promiscuous King of Olympus spoke of his sweet wish to make love to his wife, Hera.

This is a moving yearning, as old and universal as man himself. Obscene language has an old expression for it: the desire to *fuck.* This expression, like all its siblings in obscenity, has an illustrious lineage, but its etymology is uncertain. Its origin may have been from the German *ficken,* to strike; or perhaps from the Latin *pungo,* to prick; or it may be an offshoot of the French *foutre,* to thrust, which is derived from the Latin *futuare.* Although it is difficult to trace the history of the usage of this word, it seems to date back to the 15th century in Scotland.[2] It is the expression chosen by popular wit to speak of the most powerful desire in man, the one that endows him with an ineffable voluptuousness, and the one that keeps our species alive and well.

Only a weak substitute for it is tolerated by the harsh censorship, and thus we are allowed to refer to this immortal drive as *coitus.*

This is a word psychoanalysts have widely employed in their works, but it is a scientific word, and as such it is chaste and cold. It is obviously impossible to use it in a love exchange. How ludicrous it would be to invite a woman to have *coitus*! Instead, how virile and lustful it is to say, "Let's *fuck*!"

However, the taboo on words, though primitive and anachronistic, has its own logic and its own method. *To fuck* expresses the instinctive yearning in a visual way, truthful and salacious. Coitus, on the contrary, is merely an anesthetized version. It is only in this way, without its erotic splendor, that the conscience accepts instinct. Only in a faint and frigid voice is passion allowed to reach freedom and expression.

II

A subtle question has often been asked in regard to love matters: "What satisfies most when making love: touch, words, or sight?"[3] The answer is not too difficult. It is certain that there can be no pleasure without touching, but it is also true that desire is enhanced by looking and also talking. In short, to see, hear, and touch constitute the usual way of lovers. To watch and suck the tits, to caress and kiss the ass, to shit and piss in company, to suck the cock, to jerk each other off–all these pleasures, named by the scandalous list of "dirty" words, should be enjoyed at will.

An anecdote from the writer, Brantôme, who portrayed French society of his time with great fondness and boldness, illustrates this point. There were at the time many husbands among the Christians who did not wish to resemble the Turks who, it was said, felt no pleasure in gazing at their wives' cunts. So, to differentiate themselves completely, they engaged in looking at it unhurriedly and devotedly. Their loving devotion led them to kiss it with great enthusiasm. This was a habit that was quite widespread, and very well accepted by women. Thus, when the lover of a certain lady told her, "I kiss your hands, and your feet, my lady," he was confronted with the frank response, "Sir, halfway is the best site."[4]

This anecdote suggests a lesson. For joyful lovers, nothing should be forbidden–in word or in deed. Everything should be allowed. It is only in the frank flow of every erotic inclination and in their free oral expression that the full satisfaction of orgasm is achieved.

Fucking should never become a habit. The art of making desire develop and grow until maximum tension occurs is what all true lovers seek; the more the tension, the deeper the joy. Hence, the almost routine regularity of coitus that is often part of married life becomes a powerful foe to pleasure. Where there is no adventure there is no tension. On this peculiarity of the sexual instinct lies the true problem of every husband. Only the ones who successfully solve this problem grant a lasting bliss to their marriage. Indeed, as psychoanalysts have demonstrated, "marital fidelity requires a greater demand of energy than the most active of polygamous exigencies."[5]

III

All previous kinds of pleasure harmoniously resound during coitus. Yet also, sometimes, old frustrations disturbingly break into our minds. Psychoanalysis is quite familiar with them, since they have formed a major area of interest and research.

Thus, for example, psychoanalysts early perceived that there was a close connection between the problem of urinary incontinence in childhood and the later development in men of the problem of premature ejaculation. Our early conflicts always leave a lasting imprint. These men, it was discovered, cannot control their semen discharge as they could not control their urine. Moreover, typically they are subjected to frightening parents, and as children they literally piss on themselves out of fear. A patient of mine who suffered from premature ejaculation told me that as a child he felt like a little dog pissing scared whenever he was in front of his strict father.

Traumatizing childhood situations are also the source of the opposite kind of impotence: delayed ejaculation. In this disorder, the penis remains stiff throughout sexual intercourse, but orgasm is not achieved. Ferenczi used to say that the only beneficiary of this symptom was the impotent man's wife.[6] It is interesting to note that men suffering from this infrequent disorder typically have long periods of constipation during childhood, and sometimes even during later stages in their lives. That is, they cannot dispose of their semen, in much the same way that as children they could not dispose of their feces.

There is then, in both kinds of impotence, an unconscious identification between urine, feces, and semen, so much so that the disgust experienced with the first two also besmirches the third. Hence for these men, to *fuck* is not much different from shitting or pissing. It is a dirty act, and the woman who surrenders to such contemptible pleasure gets hopelessly stained. This is the idea that inspires, for example, a poem from a Spanish "Cancionero":

> Did I sin last night
> that, when the light was already off,
> after having done the sign of the cross,
> in this bed lying,
> I took, half asleep,
> my hand to my genitals
> and I started to caress them
> and to tickle them without stopping,
> so the game finally ended
> with me filled with filth?[7]

Needless to say, as adults these people do not usually suffer from either incontinence or constipation but have transferred their conflicting past attitudes to coitus. Past urethral and anal disorders then are manifested in their genitalia.

The aforesaid applies to ejaculation, but the analysis of the phenomenon of erection will allow us to integrate our findings and understand more deeply the psychology of *fucking,* and in particular, the problem of male impotence. The source of this problem is not hard to trace. As usual, popular language, intuitive and deep, leads us to the solution.

It is evident that the erect penis is a firm organ, hard, and determined. It should not be surprising, then, that men who suffer from impotence are often shy and weak, in spite of attempts they sometimes make to hide it. It is significant to note that adjectives used to characterize these poor fellows are the same as those attached to an impotent penis: weak, feeble, chicken-hearted, wrinkled, shrunk. After all, is it not common to say of a cowardly man that he is a man who "shrinks"? All this is so because the cock is always a "double" of the man. Perhaps it is even more accurate to say that the man himself is but a duplicate of it.

Psychoanalytic experience is quite eloquent on the matter. In the course of therapy, as a patient rids himself from his sexual inhibitions and recovers his initiative and erotic drive, not only his personality but also the consistency of his cock are modified. Both become stronger, harder, more penetrating and aggressive; in short, more powerful. The social behavior of a man betrays the characteristics of his sexual life. After all, do we not sometimes say of a man that he has a "penetrating" intelligence or that he is a "daring" fellow? Or that so-and-so never "shrinks"? Or that a certain person is of "good standing"? Here again, popular language reveals some simple, underlying truths.

And what about the woman? Let us consider for a moment some aspects of her physiology and psychology in this area.

The smooth muscles of the woman's vagina "seem to imitate with its spasmodic contractions as well as with its peristalsis, the oral pleasure of swallowing and the anal pleasure of retention."[8] Vulgar wisdom is also clever in this case. It subtly acknowledges this oral element in vaginal pleasure, and expresses it in the obscene phrase: "That filly 'swallows' any cock."

Indeed, the disorder known as vaginismus is characterized by muscular spasms that prevent the penis from getting out of the vagina. Anal technique prevails here. The vagina is "constipated" and traps the penis within. These are the very few cases of *penis captivus.*[9] Thus, a woman who cannot shit, enjoying the sensation of a solid turd passing through her ass, will also not be able to concentrate properly on the hard cock coming into and out of her cunt. In addition, a woman who is morally inhibited from sucking the cock will not be able to develop fully her capacity to suck it with her cunt.

It is in this way that the genital act expresses a woman's entire sexual history. This is so because *fucking,* for both sexes, is but the climax of a long and tricky route for the sexual instinct. Whatever harm moral prohibition inflicts along the way will leave painful imprints on the soul. Instead, only full freedom allows desire to acknowledge and follow faithfully its instinctive fate.

IV

The ban on uttering dirty words shows now, as it never has before, its noxious fruits.

Obscene words have a great capacity for summoning emotions. They awaken passion. If the human being does not use them, he prevents himself from experiencing vividly and truly his sexual nature. He hampers the harmonious evolution of his erotic life. He frustrates the spontaneous integration of all the manifestations of instinct in the supreme blossoming of orgasm.

To reach ecstasy in a natural fashion it is necessary, then, to break the silence, and to speak obscenely. It is necessary to *suck* and not just to kiss, to name the *cock* and not the penis, to praise the *cunt* and not the vulva. Over 2000 years ago Ovidio said in his *Ars Amatoria* (2 B.C.):

> May a woman feel even her marrow
> melt with pleasure, and search for the final
> mutual joy as well.
>
> May the caressing voices and whispers
> of happiness never stop: may never lascivious
> invocations be absent in your recreations.[10]

Lustful women over the ages have always appreciated this truth. The philosopher, Friedrich Nietzsche, admitted that the obscene talk of his lover, Lou Andreas-Salomé (1861–1937), the famous psychoanalyst, had a racy flavor that made his epigrams sound absolutely insipid.[11] Also, the 16th century writer, Brantôme, a true source of such indelicate information, confides that he loved to be "seen, touched, tasted and embraced by his lovers, turning them on with salacious speeches, impetuous words and lubricious phrases."[12]

Words have always been an optimum vehicle to kindle desire. As a further example, we note that Roman courtiers of the *seicento* mocked the great Roman ladies who did not master the use of obscene language. They said about them that *chiavano come cani, ma che sono quiete della bocca come sassi*[13] (they *fuck* as bitches but are dumb as stones).

The significance of "dirty" words in the art of love-making is also shown by the fact that sexual pleasure decreases when one *fucks* with a foreign woman who speaks a different language.

Undoubtedly, obscene words are an aphrodisiac. Hence the taboo on "dirty" words entails violence to our love life. It harms its integrity. That was Freud's view, as expressed in *On General Degradation of Erotic Life* (1912). He indicated that in order to avoid impotence, it was necessary not to adhere to the ban on uttering passionate obscenities to a woman. He stated:

> Although it may seem unpleasant, and besides, paradoxical, it can be claimed that to be able to be truly free, and thus totally happy in erotic life, it is necessary to have lost respect for the woman.[14]

V

Yet, what is the ultimate purpose guiding the eternal longing to *fuck*? What is the secret yearning that stubbornly leads men and women over time and space to merge in a loving embrace?

Psychoanalytic research on the unconscious has provided an unsuspected reply. It has come to it, above all, by elucidating the meaning of symbols. The understanding of this archaic language has yielded astonishing data.

One of the typical symbols is that of water. The sea, for example, is a proverbial symbol for mother. The earth mother is just a substitute for the primitive mother of all living creatures: the water of the sea.[15] The symbol of water stands for birth. Psychoanalysis of dreams confirms this repeatedly. So do the collective dreams of mankind: legends and myths.

In this connection, it is interesting to look at a myth which we might call "the birth of the hero." Otto Rank (1884–1939), a Viennese psychoanalyst and disciple of Freud, explored this myth at some length. He noted that in mythological accounts, it is common to find that the hero, immediately after birth, is left by himself in a basket in some body of water. He is exposed to extreme danger. But somehow, against all odds, he is rescued by alien people or by animals.[16]

Such was the case of Sargon I, the founder of Babylon, in the most ancient myth passed on to us; also, with Moses' birth as related in the Bible; and with Karna's birth, as told in the ancient Hindu Epic. Likewise, Oedipus – who according to some narratives that differ from Sophocles's tragedy – was left inside a chest in the sea; also, Perseus, born to Zeus and Danae, was locked in a coffer, together with his mother, and thrown into the sea; and, Romulus and Remus, founders of Rome, were rescued from the water by a she-wolf who suckled them and took care of them.[17]

All these mythological stories and legends on birth would seem to lead to the interpretation that the basket, chest, or coffer is a symbol for the uterus; and similarly, the water in which the hero is thrown, represents his mother's amniotic fluid where he had been living during her pregnancy. Thales of Miletus (c. 636–546 B.C.), one of the Seven Sages of Greece, and the one with whom Greek philosophy begins, must also have been thinking – though unconsciously – of this fluid when he stated that water was the source and origin of all living things.[18]

The fact that water is a symbol of birth is very suggestive. For, we also know that swimming, floating, and flying—in myths and in dreams—are symbolic expressions of both the sexual act, and the experience of being within the uterus![19] We are thus led to an intriguing question: Could it be that the ultimate goal of fucking is to go back to our mother's womb?

VI

"O paradiso dall'onde uscito, fiorente suol . . ." (Oh paradise born from waters, blossomed land . . .), so does the tenor sing in the gorgeous aria from *L'Africaine* (1865), by Meyerbeer (1791–1864), great lord of the opera of the last century.

Water and flowers are precisely the proper images of paradise since they constitute the most exquisite symbols for a woman. They represent her uterus and her cunt; that is, her genitals. There is where a man's true paradise is found. Such is the reason why a pregnant woman awakens such delicious and deep desires. Her large and full womb reminds us, unconsciously, of our own "paradise lost."

It is, certainly, amazing to discover that this is the essence of *fucking*: To get into a female's womb, and thereby return to our mother's womb. Indeed, the intimate sensations in the lovers' souls during the dialogue between their bodies, reveals the hidden purpose of this instinctive yearning. It is a yearning as old as the history of man. Mention of it can be found in the Hindu *Upanishad,* the most ancient psychology of our race:

> Holding her beloved, man forgets the whole world: what is within and what is without it.[20]

And similarly in the well-known prophecy from the Bible (Genesis 2:24):

> . . . shall a man leave his father and his mother, and shall cleave unto his wife: and they shall be one flesh.[21]

Already Plato, speaking through Aristophanes, in 400 B.C., had perceived that the stubborn aim of desire was to overcome the boundaries of the body:

> He believed he had just heard what he had yearned for since so long ago on coupling and melting with the beloved: to become one out of two.[22]

In sum, *fucking* undoubtedly involves the craving to be merged with the other. Man wants to get into a woman, and a woman wants to feel him within her. And this is the most intimate communion granted by nature to those who love each other. Do we not say of lovers that they are "wrapped up in each other"?

In fact, the cock achieves this merging. It gets into the loved body, and as it is characteristic of every healthy man—as Freud pointed out—to identify himself with his sexual member, he feels it is he himself who gets in.[23] In the unconscious, the phallus is a person in itself, so much so that it has been given names and nicknames. In Colombia it is called "Carlitos"; in Cuba, "Pepe"; in Mexico, "Sancho"; in Chile, "Pepito"; in Peru, "Juanito."[24] That is why vaginal coitus is not only necessary but also indispensable; only through it can we, temporarily, overcome the limits of our flesh.

Yet, *fucking* grants even another, more intimate reward. The joyous man does not identify himself only with his cock, but with his semen as well. And during ecstasy, when his semen flows, he feels he himself is also melting. It is not his semen, but he who gets dissolved.

Thus, Socrates (469–399 B.C.) says in *Banquet* I, 206, that when the lover possessed by love "has the urge to beget, he tries to find something beautiful, he relaxes, and spills himself, procreates, and begets."[25]

Indeed, it is thus how, at last, on "flowing among delights," that man in his new voluptuous identity can reach *ad litteram,* literally, the craved for waters.

VII

But, what happens to a woman?

It is obvious that she has also been within the uterus and that, therefore, she too wishes to go back to it. Nature, however, has denied her this indescribable pleasure. It is man's privilege. Yet, nature has granted her another incomparable joy. Her mission is not to enter but to receive. She does not get in, she lodges. That is why rooms, corridors, and houses are typical female representations in dreams.

She finds joy in sheltering man. True, she sometimes feels her guest only in a more limited way, as when, with the man's hard cock inside her, she whispers: "I feel *it* deep inside me." But, as such, her delicate essence is not unveiled. It reveals itself only when the feeling awakened in her is transferred from it alone to the whole of her lover's body. Only then does she welcome him completely. This is the delicious moment when, thrilled, she tells him: "I feel *you* deep inside me."

However, the truly entrancing moment comes when the man leaves his seed inside her. Then, she belongs to him. She holds his seed and treasures it. That is why she does not want him to withdraw from her cunt after ejaculation. While keeping within herself both his penis and his semen, it is as if she is already holding the child in her womb. For her, man, cock, semen, and child constitute, profoundly, one single being. And all of them does she cover with the warm mantle of her womb. She is the sea.

VIII

Alexandre Dumas, *fils* (1824–1895), in his famous novel *Dame aux Camélias* (1852) perceived, unconsciously, in captivating pages, that *fucking* meant a going back to primeval waters. He describes in his novel those two unforgettable lovers, Margarithe Gauthier and Armand Duval, who lived in Eden-like bliss in the country. Margarithe was, for Armand, the core of creation. They were forever longing to be in each other's arms. They would prolong this intimacy over whole days. And then after

> those exhausting experiences we used to fall asleep, paying no mind to the time of day, but since love is always willing to keep awake, it turned out that sleep was short and light, and in this we were like divers, who go up to the surface just long enough to get their breath back.[26]

Being under water! Being a diver! It is not possible to express better the deep experience of *fucking.* We were born from the water and to the water we want to return. Out of this inexhaustible longing is born, too, the aesthetic pleasure aroused when, in Homer's words, we behold the *Polyphloisboio Thallases,* the sea of many waves.

IX

The "tedious monotony" with which the incestuous desire towards the mother arises repeatedly during the therapy of male patients becomes comprehensible now.[27] This yearning is none other than the wish to return to her womb. One of the worst insults men can exchange, *"You mother fucker,"* is thus rather ambiguous. After all, that is precisely what all men want to do after they are born! And the "dirty" word, *to fuck,* always means, at root, to *fuck* one's mother; to go back to her womb. Such is the universal Oedipus longing. Therefore its frank and spontaneous use in everyday life would threaten to bring to consciousness the "sleeping dogs" among fathers and sons.[28] In sum, the ban on the "dirty" word *fuck* aims at completely burying the universal incestuous desire.

But this desire cannot be banned. Disease is always the price for such an arbitrary gesture. Schopenhauer, who anticipated so many of the discoveries of psychoanalysis, knew this very well: "The true sanity of the spirit is but the perfect remembrance of the past."[29] Only through "dirty" words can we recall and faithfully express something of this passion. That is why they must have their rightful place in every sane society, and for every sane man and woman.

9

THE VOLUPTUOUS MOTHER

"May you burn to ashes, since such an old whore as your mother was I."

FERNANDO DE ROJAS
(The Celestine, Act I, 1499)

I
PRELUDE

Along a street in Salamanca, in Seville, or in Toledo, a citizen strolls. Suddenly, someone sees her and shouts, "old *whore*," and the woman, who is not only old but also bearded, without any embarrassment, turns around and answers with a happy face.[1] Her name is the Celestine; she is a sorceress, astute, full of strategems. She is also a *whore*. We know that the character was born out of Fernando de Rojas' pen but nobody knows, however, the age of the profession. It is an old business. And the obscene word that names such ancient workers is one of those most frequently used. In the obscene phrase, *son of a whore,* mother and concupiscence are mingled in a disturbing way. It is one of the most suggestive "dirty" words, and with its analysis we arrive at the end of our journey through the world of taboo words.

II
AN ANCIENT PROFESSION

"Eutique the Greek, willing to please, offers herself for two aces."

POMPEIAN AMATORY GRAFFITI
(Advertisement of a Prostitute)

It has been said that man is different from other animals in that he eats without being hungry, drinks without being thirsty and makes love in all seasons. Since sexual desire is untiring, whores have always helped men to get rid of the necessity that knows no season. There is almost no society where prostitutes cannot be found. In Egypt, during the reign of the Ptolemies, one such lady managed to construct a pyramid.[2] In Babylon, their skills were famous. Many of them lived inside the temple and there were also those who amassed, patiently, large fortunes. *Whores* were also to be found, in the ancient world, throughout West Asia in Lydia, Cyprus, Phoenicia, and Phrygia. In Judea, because law appeared not to prohibit relations with foreign *whores,* Syrian, Moabite and Midianite women offered themselves in shacks, tents, and stables, along the royal roads.[3]

In Greece, practices were not much different. In Athens, it constituted a promising profession, with several varied specialties and ranks. The lowest ones were the *pornai.* They lived in gloomy brothels by the harbor in Piraeus, where they exhibited their merchandise by means of their transparent tunics. A higher position was occupied by the *auletridas* or flute players who, like the Japanese *geishas,* did not have any prejudice, during stag parties where they entertained, against occasionally changing the instrument. At the top of the profession were the *heteras* companions. They received their guests in their own homes. Teoris, Arquipa, Danae, Lais, and Aspasia provided solace, relief, and education to such illustrious men as the playwright, Sophocles (496?–406? B.C.), the philosophers, Epicurus (341–270 B.C.) and Aristippus (435?–356? B.C.), and the statesman, Pericles (499–429 B.C.).[4]

Friné, perhaps the most beautiful, used to conceal her body, even her hair, behind the folds of a charming veil. For some time she loved Praxiteles (towards 340 B.C.), who left her immortal shape in the sculpture, *Aphrodite of Cnido,* and then Apelles (towards 330 B.C.), who, inspired by her body, painted his *Anadiodema* (Aphrodite coming out from the sea).[5] She amassed so large a fortune that she offered to reconstruct the city walls of Thebes if her name were engraved on the stones–a gesture that the inhabitants of the city refused to accept.

In Rome, prostitution was also a vigorous trade. The brothels had acquired such a reputation that certain politicians organized their electoral campaign by means of the *collegium lupanorum,* the guild of whorehouse proprietors.[6] These establishments opened their doors on the dark corners of the city suburbs or at roadsides, where exhausted travelers found at the *mansio* or inn satisfaction of all their appetites.[7] They were patronized by some of the most distinguished personalities. Emperor Domitian (51–96), for example, democratically took baths with them.[8]

During the Middle Ages, prostitution had to adapt to hard times. And so it did, with even an occasional convent serving to give the old profession a new look. Accordingly, warnings were issued, one after the other: Charlemagne (724–814) ordained a strict surveillance to prevent prostitution among nuns;[9] Bishop Ivo de Chartres (1035–1115) found it at Saint Fara's monastery; Abélard (1079–1142), the castrated monk, also knew about these acts among some French Carthusian nuns; and Pope Innocent III (1161–1216) described Saint Agatha's abbey as a whorehouse.[10]

Gayer times and less austere settings were to follow. During the Renaissance in Rome, and in Venice, for example, prostitution was carried on with enterprising commercial spirit; edited catalogues with names, addresses, and prices became part of the business. The finest *cortigiane oneste* (whores) competed with the most distinguished ladies in dress, manners, and culture.[11] Many of them, stimulated by the Greek and Roman tradition, adopted classical names: Camila, Polixena, Pontisilea, or Tulia. Imperia of Cugnatis was the model for Raphael's (1483–1520) Sappho of Parnassus; and the death of the famous Faustina Mancina anguished half of Rome, causing even Michelangelo (1475–1564)–who was usually more sensitive to virile muscles than to feminine flesh–to write a sonnet in her memory.[12]

One could go on and on detailing the varied history of this longstanding profession. But suffice it to say, simply, that some of these women, probably most, led wretched lives and attended their clients in gloomy surroundings, while a few enjoyed opulence and lodged at sumptuous mansions; that they were frequented by some of the most despicable men, and also some of the most illustrious; and that on occasion they offered their bodies as models to the greatest artists and their talent as incentive to the most outstanding thinkers. And finally, though we do not easily think of them in this light, some of these lewd women had sons – men who, logically, we call *sons of whores.*

As for these latter fellows, soon we will deal with them.

III
VIRGIN MOTHERS

> *"The legend which tells us that Latin kings were born from virgin mothers and divine fathers, becomes a little more intelligible, for tales of that sort, isolated from their fabulous elements, signify, no more, no less, that a woman has been made pregnant by a stranger."*
>
> *SIR JAMES FRAZER*
> (*The Golden Bough, Chapter XIV, 1922*)

That a whore can have a son is a natural fact. It is something implicit in the natural order of things: a man goes to bed with a woman and a son is born. It is incomprehensible that a woman who has not had sexual intercourse can have a baby. The notion of a virgin mother is simply preposterous – at least in the world as we know it. Where it is possible to find a virgin mother, of course, is in fantasies or in dreams. In the imaginary world everything is possible. And there, certainly, we do often find virgin mothers. Indeed, the myth of the virgin mother is a very old one.

Let us look for a moment at some of these myths.

Chigemouni, the Mongol Savior, chose the most perfect virgin on the earth, Mahaenna o Maya, and impregnated her by penetrating her right ear.[13] The same anatomical spot was used by Surya, the solar Hindu god, to fecundate the untouched princess, Hunti, and to bring Karma to the world.[14] In Egypt, Pharaoh Amenophis' chaste mother became pregnant by means of the hot breath of celestial fire.[15] The Phrygians also had a miraculously born hero: Atis, who had been conceived by the virgin Nana when she put an almond or a pomegranate between her tits.[16]

In Greek mythology, too, various versions of a virgin birth can be found. For example, the oracle of Delphi told Acriso, ruler of Argos, that he would be killed by his grandson. Thus, in order to avoid this fatal design, the king locked his daughter, Danae, in an iron tower; there no male could touch her. In solitary confinement, she spent her days consumed with sorrow. But it happened that Zeus, moved by the tears of the sad virgin, decided to comfort her. He transformed himself into a golden rain, and thus wetted her delicious flesh. From this immaculate conception, Perseus came into life, but Danae's father, who did not believe her story, locked her together with the baby in a trunk and threw them both into the sea.[17]

Some Greek philosophers were also said to be the offspring of celestial parents. For instance, the last disciples of Pythagoras (6 B.C.) believed him to be a son of Apollo.[18] Also, it was thought that Plato's grandson, Speuzipo, was the son of the beautiful virgin, Perictiona, and of the god of light, since Ariston, her husband, had not touched her before the delivery.[19]

Alexander the Great (356–323 B.C.) was said to have had a similar origin. His mother Olympia, in the middle of a thunderstorm, was struck by lightning in her womb. She was still a virgin. Later, her husband, Philip, after consummating the marriage, had a dream in which he seemed to seal his wife's womb, and the seal had the image of a lion engraved on it. The seers who were consulted reassured him that the image solely referred to the fact that the king should watch over his wife more carefully. But Aristandrus of Telmisio claimed that the dream meant that his wife was pregnant, because what was empty needs no sealing; and further, that the boy would be courageous like a lion. Olympia, anyway, decided for reasons of her own to tell Alexander that he was the son of Zeus, who during a dark and rainy night had penetrated her with his lightning.[20]

Similarly, there were Romans said to have been born from virgin mothers and divine fathers. The twins, Romulus and Remus (8th century B.C.), were said to be the sons of the union between the maiden, Rhea Silvia – who had "opened her breasts to catch the breeze"[21] – and the god, Mars. So, too, did the first Scipio ascribe his birth to the union of Jupiter with his mother.[22] And, equally divine was Augustus' birth (63 B.C.–14 A.D.). Acia, his mother, Suetonius tells us in *Octav*, XCIV:

> having gone at midnight to Apollo's temple for a solemn sacrifice, she fell asleep in the litter while the other women were marching; then a serpent slid over her side and it left a moment later; when she woke up she purified herself as if she had come out of her husband's arms, and since then she had in her body the image of a

> serpent which she never could delete so that she never wanted to show herself in public baths; and Augustus, who was born nine months later, was considered, for this reason, as Apollo's son.[23]

In Jewish history, too, one can find the myth of virgin births. For example, during the reign of King Arcaz, the kings of Syria and Israel were on their way to war against Judah. Arcaz begged, trembling, for the help of the Assyrians, and it was then that the prophet, Isaiah, calmed him by saying that as proof that God was by his side, a maiden would conceive and give birth to a son by the name of Emmanuel, or "God is with us."[24]

For their part, the Christians had Mary. The angel of the Lord had announced that the shadow of God would fall upon her and that her womb would bear fruit. The girl became pregnant. When her husband, Joseph, learned about this, he wanted to abandon her, but Gabriel, the messenger of God, appeared in his dreams and persuaded him that Mary was pregnant by an act of the Holy Spirit. Then Joseph, moved, did not have sex with her during her pregnancy.[25] And thus was Jesus born.

How exactly did the divine conception of Jesus happen? According to a deeply rooted tradition of the Church, it was by the introduction of the Holy Spirit through her ear. Saint Augustine (354–430) (*Sermo de Tempore*, XXII) is peremptory about this matter: "Deus per angelum loquebatur et Virgo per aurem impraegnebatur"[26] ("God by means of the angel's voice and through the virgin's ear impregnated her").

Sometimes the Holy Spirit is represented by a dove; sometimes by an angel that has wings. The subject, in the Middle Ages, was painted by many artists: Ambrogio Lorenzetti (?–1348) at Siena's Pinacotheca, and Simone

Martini (1285–1344) at Ambere's Royal Museum of Art, represented the fecundating bird flying towards the Madonna. And in Fra Filippo Lippi's (1406–1469) paintings at the convent of Saint Mark in Florence, in Gaddi's (1300–1366) in Saint Maria Novella, and in Benozzo Gozzoli's (1424–1498) at Campo Santo in Pisa, the bird is almost entering through her ear. But in Martini's *Annunciation,* which is at the Uffizi Gallery in Florence, the breath sent by the angel, without any mediation, enters her directly.

We could go on and on, of course, with examples of these legendary virgin births, but let us stop here and see if we can analyze some of this mythological material. If we examine it closely, it seems that there are some common threads.

There are many legends but they are all variations on the same theme. For example, with the Mongolian Mahaenna, the Hindu Hunti, and the Christian Mary, impregnation was through the ear; or, in the case of Amenophis, impregnation was by means of the celestial breath. And very often, it is some god who "fathers" the child. Thus, each of the girls, Mahaenna, Hunti, Danae, Perictiona, Olympia, Rhea Silvia, Acia, and Mary were virgins made pregnant by gods.

The myths are many but the story is one; a story reiterated almost obsessively throughout history and in different places. And this is very interesting because its fabulous characteristics conceal as well as reveal. The story assures a virginal conception. It affirms a fact that violates the laws of nature, but at the same time denies it. This is strange, but also comprehensible. For, as Freud teaches us, it is not typical of human beings to keep a secret. The legend originates in the unconscious of man, and the unconscious always speaks its truth; although it does so in its own language of symbols and allusions. Its suggestions are unmistakable: What else are the serpent that slid over Acia, the lightning that penetrated Olympia, the dust that left Danae pregnant, the dove that flew over Mary, the red pomegranate that Nana put between her breasts, if not classical representations of the phallus?

The long serpent that stretches and shrinks like the penis is perhaps its universal symbol, and the "lightning"of the master of the world, as the Latins knew in their dissolute poems,[27] is none other than the obscene "weapon" that the god carries between his legs. The "bird" that visited Mary is the consecrated symbol behind which, under the shape of a dove, Jupiter shielded himself in order to seduce Phtheia during one of his love expeditions.[28] And finally, the pomegranate that Nana puts between her tits reminds us with its red color of the erect penis.

In addition, the receptive ear of Mahaenna, Hunti, and Mary would seem to be a fancy disguise for the vulva. The ear, with its soft and smooth lobe, and the folds of its pavilion that surround and determine the orifice of the auditory canal, does indeed suggest the anatomical structure of the cunt. Thus, it should not surprise us that Molière (1622–1673) leaves on Agnes' lips, in his *Ecole des Femmes* (Act V, Scene 4), the naive question of whether sons are made through the ear; and Rabelais has his ineffable Gargantua born through the same orifice.[29]

What are repressed, the phallus and the vagina, return masked in the myth. The same legend that consciously speaks about virginity, unconsciously refers to coitus. The manifest subject, as in dreams, covers up a latent one that is not only opposite but also incompatible.

Historical reality is different from what myth proclaims: there were not virgin mothers because a man always made them pregnant.

Sir James Frazer says that tales of this sort become more comprehensible when it is noticed that at heart they signify that a woman has been made pregnant by a stranger. A man has existed but his identity is unknown. Such an interpretation is certainly plausible, but it is also possible that another interpretation, which does not contradict it, also sheds further light. Namely, what if the man was not a stranger? Perhaps he was known, but was excluded, his existence denied.

The myth, then, would not be the result of ignorance but of repression. Let us continue.

IV
TWO FACES AND ONE WOMAN

"The common infantile fantasy of one's mother being virginal signifies a repudiation of any part played by the father in one's birth and the jealous distaste felt at the idea of sexual intercourse between the parents."

ERNEST JONES
(Psycho-analysis and Christian Religion, 1930)

Man has known, since the beginning, about the existence of *whores* and virgins. He also has heard that both can have sons. Obviously, it is difficult to imagine two more opposite mothers, two more distant females. Yet, perhaps, the distance is just an illusion, and the two are not so distant after all? Perhaps, the two women, the *whore* mother and the virgin mother, correspond–in the psyche of man–to one and the same woman?

The wish to possess one's own mother is universal. So is its prohibition. "Mom is mine!" exclaims the little boy while stretching against her familiar breasts. The gesture supposes a challenge; his father is his rival. He is the man who, every night in bed, enjoys the mother and her charming warmth, whereas the boy, in that bed, is only an alien, an occasional guest. It is true that, sometimes, he breaks in at night and gets cozy by her side, but it is also true that, sooner or later, he is put back in his own bed.

If a man catches his woman lying down with another man, he will react, surely, with hatred and violence, unless fear inhibits him, or unless he is perverse. This is so dramatic an event that, understandably, it represents a common theme in novels and plays. As Othello (Act III, Scene III, 267–270) put it:

> I had rather be a toad
> And live upon the vapor of a dungeon
> Than keep a corner in the thing I love
> For others' uses.

But what can the little boy, in such a position, do about it? Nothing at all. His small size restrains him from a valiant response. So, what attitude does the small Othello adopt? He denies it! He unconsciously lies to himself and in the bizarre effort he adulterates reality. The voluptuous mother is discarded from his mind, and the mother who remains is solely chaste and tender. Lustful spasms of the flesh no longer exist for her. In fact, he even begins to tell himself that they never existed! She was always pure. But if this is so, how was he born? He was born without Father's having touched her. Mom is virgin!

Denial is, in fact, the source of myth.

Only a fantasy shared by a vast number of people acquires the consolidated shape of a myth or legend. The venerable Mongol, Hindu, Phrygian, Egyptian, Greek, Roman, Jewish, and Christian tales could be repeated *ad infinitum,* since there exist as many virgin mothers as there are sons. The infantile belief in the virgin mother is so strongly rooted in the child's soul that its unmistakable vestiges can be distinguished in any adult: nobody has an image of his mother *fucking*! In everyone, a persistent mist engulfs the love life of his parents. As regards this, there is no one who has well-defined ideas. Patients repeatedly tell us: "Nothing comes to my mind"; "They were so cold"; "Mom did not like it"; "They never did it"; "I cannot even imagine them"; "They were into something else." In this kind of silent conspiracy the conclusion is, in short, only one: *mom did not fuck.*

But if the virgin mother is a fantasy, the *whore* mother is real. Every mother is for her son, unconsciously, a *whore,* due to the fact that she deserts him for his father. She is lustful and promiscuous; thus, in his unconscious, she is a *whore.* Indeed, the image of his parents fucking is carried in the depths of every man's soul. This vision is so important that psychoanalysis has introduced a special name for it: the primal scene. Freud thought that it was an inherited patrimony, a heritage of the species.[30]

A famous patient of his, "The Wolf Man," observed his parents *fucking* like wild beasts, when he was only one and a half years old! The little boy, who suffered from malarial fever, was in his room. It was a summer day. He was sleeping in his cradle and they were lying on the bed almost naked. They were caressing one another during that hot siesta. And then they were joined in one of the voluptuous ways which Ovid sings (*Artis Amoris*, III, 781–782):

> Be the mattress well pressed against
> the knees
> slightly bent the neck,
> by that who has the beauty in the
> length of her flank.

What can so young a child understand? This is the typical reasoning of parents. That is why it is not unusual, during psychoanalysis, to uncover buried memories of such scenes. They belong, generally, to early childhood, since the older the child, the more the parents take care not to exhibit themselves. A patient of mine, a young and sensuous woman, told me that one morning after finishing *fucking* with her husband, she realized that her one-year-and-seven-month-old daughter, who was sleeping in the same bedroom, was standing up in the cradle, her eyes wide open and watching the show!

Lascivious poses are, supposedly, the specialty of prostitutes. However, the nine positions which the poetess Elephantis enumerated in ancient times, and the sixteen poses which Giulio Romano (1498–1556) painted during the Renaissance, are no more than copies of those which are spontaneously adopted by any woman who yields herself to her passion. Here, privileges do not exist because it is instinct that, democratically, inspires all of them. That is why the mother, when she performs them during the primal scene, is merely demonstrating her genuine attributes as a *whore.*

Poets just record what the female creates. Thus, the Greek Aristophanes (?448–?380 B.C.) in *The Peace*, V, 889–890:

> So that it is possible, lifting up her legs,
> to accomplish, up high, the mysteries

or in the *Birds*, V, 1255,

> . . . the messenger first lifts up her legs
> and I pierce her

or in *Lysistrata*, 667

> Women are fond of riding a horse
> and hold tight

The Roman Horace (65–8 B.C.) in his *Satires*, II, 7–49, also contributes:

> . . . naked, under the bright lamp
> she tramples lasciviously with her
> buttocks on the fallen horse

And there is still the presence of Lucretius (?99–?55 B.C.) (*De Rerum Natura*, IV, 1259):

> . . . in the beast-way it is considered
> that women conceive better.

Some of these positions are observed by the son during the primal scene, his first *porno show.* They leave in his spirit the desire to see them again. The mother in her lustful poses is recorded forever in the child's mind. This unconscious memory will compel him, when he reaches adulthood, to search for women who will repeat them. So it was that "The Wolf Man," who as a child saw his father *fucking* his mother from the rear, as an adult had a predilection for women crouched and giving their *ass.*

The mother is an example for everything. The virgin mother is an illusion, but the *whore* mother is real.

V
THE POWER OF A SMILE

> *"Begin, oh tender child!, to know your mother by her smile; for ten months she has carried you inside her womb with grave zeal; begin, oh tender child."*
>
> *VIRGIL*
> *(Eclogues, IV, 60–64)*

The illusion of a virgin mother is pernicious. It constitutes the source of severe disorders in the love life of man. Impotence is the most conspicuous. Under the rubric of impotence, we can also include those men who are potent with women they despise, but impotent with those they respect, as well as those men who feel bored after *fucking* and want to expel from bed the woman whom they have just possessed. William Hogarth in his paintings *Before* and *Afterwards* gave eternal expression to this bewildering succession of emotions. Only in regard to these disturbed lovers is the false phrase true: *omne animal post coitum triste* (every animal is sad after coitus). Impotence, enlarging the concept, is almost an epidemic.[31]

The virgin mother and the *whore* mother are at odds in the soul of these men. That is why they love whom they do not desire and desire whom they do not love. They cannot feel towards one woman both passion and tenderness, just as they could not experience both these feelings with their mothers. They only will be able to weld these feelings when they give up the infantile illusion of the virgin mother, and accept that mom is a *whore*. Only when they admit that the beloved mother gets horny too, will they be able, in turn, to get horny themselves with the woman they love. The belief in the virgin mother, human or divine, is, doubtless, harmful. It distorts the genuine image of woman and, thus, our capacity for loving her. Famous examples exist.

Saint Augustine, who as a youngster revelled in the pleasures of the flesh, recalled in *The Confessions*, II, 3:

> I embarked myself with such a blindness that, among my friends, I was ashamed with guilt of showing less lewdness than them, because I heard them boasting about their brazenness, as well as they boasted about how beastly they had acted; and I found pleasure in doing it, not only for the joy of the deed itself but for the praise it gave. . . .

As an adult, he founded a religious order, lived in poverty and celibacy, and devoted himself to study and prayer. Thus, in this about-face, he reflected the contradictions in his soul. His notions about original sin, for example, are tinged unconsciously by this infantile dissociation. His theory is simple: Eve and Adam's sin is the cause of evil, and the original sin is concupiscence. Since concupiscence is inseparable from the task of making children, almost every one of us is condemned. The only ones who can be saved are those for whom Mary–who conceived without sin—intercedes. The saint differentiated absolutely between different types of women, as in *The City of God*, 289: "A woman was the cause of our ruin; another woman cleared the way for our salvation."

The split is complete: Eve, the *whore* mother, and Mary, the virgin mother. The consequences were obvious. Saint Augustine could choose only between debauchery and asceticism; between sin and sanctity. He believed there was no other option! He only knew the excesses and never learned that in love, desire and tenderness come together.

Nor did Dante and Petrarch (1304–1374) know about it. With both these poets, the dissociation was no less extreme. Dante could never even look at Beatrice, and Petrarch never spoke to Laura, but both thought they loved the women. They offered as gifts the music of their poems.

Beatrice was inimitable (*Vita Nova*, XIX):

> Dice di lei Amor: "Cosa mortale
> como esser pò sì adorna e sì pura?
> Poi la reguarda, e fra se stesso giura
> che Dio ne 'ntenda di far cosa nova.

> He says of her Love: Something mortal, how can it be so beautiful and pure? Then he looks at her, and swears to himself that God intended to do something new.

Laura, in turn, was the image of divine beauty (*Canzionere*, 159):

> Non sa come Amore sana, e come ancide,
> chi non sa come dolce ella sospira,
> e come dolce parla e dolce ride.

> He does not know how love heals and fiercely kills that who does not know how sweetly she talks, sighs and laughs.

They were beautiful but remote women; without bodies, all spirit. The extreme distinction that these two men made between voluptuousness and tenderness turned love into a painful caricature. Dante, who so delicately sang to Beatrice, had a wife and two sons to whom he did not dedicate, in all his poetry, a single word. And Petrarch, while he was rhyming melodious verses for his ethereal Laura, frequented a lover who gave him two sons. The virgin mother and the *whore* mother!

Only an internal well-established image of the *whore* mother ensures a healthy love life in the male. The reason is easily understandable: "If mom, who is good and tender, *fucks*, so can I with the woman I love!" As parents are the example for everything, the voluptuous mother not only teaches but also authorizes. She offers herself as the unconscious model upon which the son, as an adult, patterns his choices.

But if the *whore* mother stimulates, the virgin mother saddens. Is it not sadness that we generally feel in contemplating a painting or sculpture of a virgin mother, with her slightly melancholy face and an austere cloth on her head? The absence of pleasure depresses the mother—and the son! Sadness is a contagious disease. It is the price of damming up instinct.

The *whore* mother, on the other hand, is happy like any satisfied woman. As she *fucks*, she smiles, and that smile has immense power. It promises her son joyfulness, because if the mother smiles, life will likely smile on him too. As the Roman poet, Virgil (70 B.C.–19 B.C.), told us, the child who can recognize his mother by her smile will also recognize the way to the gods' table and to the goddesses' bed.[32]

In sum, then, the "dirty" expression, *son of a whore,* like all others that we have discussed, conjures up incestuous images and pleasures. Therefore, to be able to say and hear it freely, and to accept its true emotive meaning, is to be able to live with the reality it proclaims. In a word, it is to be free. Of course, it is no curse word, and not at all obscene, to call someone a *son of a virgin*; but such a fate would not be the wish of any healthy man.

10

IN PRAISE OF OBSCENITY

"Does psychoanalysis have any sound reasons to condemn incestuous relations between mother and her son? And if this were so, which are they? They cannot evidently be the reasons stemming from a simple taboo."

SIGMUND FREUD
(Letter to Marie Bonaparte, April 30, 1932)

I
TABOO

Ab uno disce omnes (from one we learn to know all). Along different paths all "dirty" words take us to the same place. All, without exception, lead us to infancy. What is true for one is true for all of them: *tit, suck tit, suck cock, ass, shit, piss, fart, have the ass, jerk off, cunt, fuck, son of a whore,* and so on. All obscene words stimulate, or threaten to stimulate, reminiscences of incestuous anguish and pleasures. Besides, they bring to mind only adult sexual organs.

That is why Voltaire so shocked us when we read his striking letter with which we began our obscene itinerary – the letter wherein he told his niece that his cock was in love with her and that he also kissed her gentle ass. The philosopher was accomplishing incest twice, so to speak. He evoked it in words, and indicated that he had already consummated it, in fact, with her.

Now we understand why censorship implacably falls upon these dreaded words. It is due to the same cause that makes us shiver when we hear them: the taboo of incest.

The clash between incestuous feelings and moral repulsion strikes a strong emotional chord and evokes a traumatic situation. All traumas, such as in dreams, provoke hallucinations. That is why "dirty" words are hallucinatory. This is their distinctive attribute. They are the offspring of awe, moral anguish, and of incestuous wishes.

The mystery, then, is revealed, but let us play with our imagination. Let us try, in our fantasy, to speak obscenely with our parents, authentically, without compromising feelings, looking at them right in the eye. It would be impossible! We would feel disturbed, uncomfortable, anxious. We would experience the same thing if somebody told them an obscene joke right in front of us. A vivid but disquieting awareness of our animal nature and of our bodies and their sensuality would invade us. Like Adam and Eve we would discover our nakedness.

An ancient and silent resolution would then shatter into pieces; the tacit agreement that goes back to tender childhood would be broken. After all, it is during childhood when parents, alert and patient, teach their curious child the words by which he can know the world: "This is called a cat," "This is a tree," and so on. In their slow and loving teaching, they incorporate into the child's mind the rudiments of language, and they stimulate the child's intelligence.

Does any father or mother employ the same solicitousness and diligence when offering their children the words that describe the world of sex? Who satisfies the child's sexual curiosity by saying, "This is called the cock"; "This is called the cunt"? Nobody, of course. Thereafter a split world is created for the child: a world of things with legitimate official names and a world that is shrouded in silence, unnamed.

There is no greater condemnation than such silence. By refusing to give names to the objects and happenings of this world, the first infantile repression is developed, since we are only conscious of what we can name. Only through words do feelings and wishes inhabiting the unconscious receive the full light of consciousness. This is the true magic of the word. By naming things we give life to them.

Psychoanalysis is based on this premise. We offer the adult, in the course of treatment, words that parents have stolen, that is, obscene words. During psychoanalysis, incestuous desires have to be remembered and intensely reexperienced. Talking is necessary to overcome the taboo, and this must be done genuinely, which means obscenely. Only in this way can instinct be made conscious. A psychoanalysis that does not help in overcoming the taboo of incest does not reach the safe harbor of sanity.

This is understandable. The "Oedipus complex" is not only the *kernkomplex,* the nodular complex of "every neurosis,"[1] but also of several organic diseases, such as myocardial infarction, asthma, ulcer, rheumatic inflammations, obesity, migraine, vomiting, and caprices. The

Spanish psychoanalyst, Angel Garma (1904), tells us in *The Psychoanalysis* (1978) that they are no more than "special elaborations"[2] of the same and deep rooted passion. The importance, then, of giving words to incestuous desires is truly immeasurable.

II

What is the origin of this ominous taboo? Prohibition of incest is universal. It is in force both in primitive and civilized societies, but its reasons are by no means so sound. In fact, there are no biological reasons to justify this prohibition. Procreation among close relatives is not necessarily harmful.[3] Besides, while the marriage between mother and son is, and has been, banned in all cultures,[4] the union between father and daughter has, on rare occasions, been permitted.

For instance, Ramses II (1300–1233 B.C.), the last of the great Egyptian pharaohs, married not only one but several of his daughters.[5] At present, this incestuous relationship is permitted at least among the Azande, a people of central Africa.[6]

Another form of incestuous pleasure–the union between siblings–has been widespread in the course of history. The Incas of ancient Peru favored marriage between siblings,[7] and among Hawaiian royal families this type of marriage was compulsory.[8] These unions were also habitual in ancient Egypt. In the 2nd century A.D., it is said that two thirds of the citizens of the province of Arsinoe enjoyed this deep fraternal intimacy.[9]

The Bible, too, informs us of similar practices. In Genesis 19:30–38, we are informed of the incestuous doings of old Lot. Depicted in the voluptuous canvas of the German painter, Albrecht Altdorfer (1480–1538), *Lot and his Daughters* (1525), we see the old man partaking of such pleasures.[10]

In the Middle Ages incest was frequent,[11] and at present it is certainly not unusual.[12] The French psychoanalyst, Marie Bonaparte (1882–1962), in her book *La Sexualité de la Femme* (1953), describes one such case–that of three girls who were successfully initiated into sex by their brothers.[13]

In our culture it is "displaced incest" that is most common. This kind of "incest" occurs when the longing is not satisfied with the desired person but with a similar one. Thus, there are young men who get married to women much older than themselves. Some of these unions are really happy, and also famous. Such is the case of the English statesman, Benjamin Disraeli (1804–1881), Lord Beaconsfield, who married a woman 16 years older than himself.[14]

Undoubtedly, the reverse situation is more common: that is, men who choose as wives women who are their daughter's age. One of the best known is that of Rubens, the renowned Flemish painter. After the death of his first wife, Elizabeth Brant, who was 14 years younger, and with whom he had three sons, he then married his best friend's daughter, a woman 37 years younger![15]

III

The facts mentioned have been, no doubt, quite illustrative but they do not exhaust our curiosity. We can still go further in our inquiry.

Why is the taboo of incest so harsh in regard to the sexual desire of a son towards his mother? What is the cause of this rule that has no exceptions? Why can a son not fuck his own mother?

If the sexual relationship between mother and son is the only one universally condemned, and instead the union between father and daughter is still tolerated in some places, it becomes apparent that the only excluded partner is the son, and the most privileged partner is the father. Since this is so, it is not too bold to state that inasmuch as the benefits of the prohibition accrue to the father, the authorship of the prohibition must be his as well.

The taboo has undoubtedly been introduced by the tyrannical father as it is he who profits from it. This is a fact that should not shock us, since we have already come across this father during our study. He is the ferocious father of the primitive human horde. The supreme prohibition is a consequence of his barbaric ways. He was a jealous and brutal male for whom his sons represented dangerous rivals. All the females were his. Women were the most valuable property of this dreadful man. So great and feared was his power that it left very deep imprints on the souls of his sons. Trails of this subduing dominion can be found, for example, in the *jus primae noctis* of the ancient Anglo-Saxons, whereby the feudal lord has the privilege of deflowering his servant girls on their wedding day.[16]

The taboo rests on this triumphant patriarchal pretension. However, the father's harshness often brings about serious consequences. Parricide, the murder of the father, is the most severe. There are those, like Diderot, who believe that the difference between the primitive and the civilized world, is such that

> if the little savage were abandoned on his own, kept all his imbecility and joined the scarce reasoning of the child in a cradle with the violence of a thirty-year-old man's passions, he would strangle his father and would have sexual intercourse with his mother.[17]

This widespread idea, however, is only a confusion generated by the very taboo. It constitutes a serious mistake. Parricide is never a consequence of incestuous desire, but of its prohibition. Filicide, that is, ill-treatment, intimidation, or killing of children, as the Argentine psychoanalyst, Arnaldo Rascovky (1907), has shown in his book *Filicide* (1973), always precedes parricide.[18] And the prohibition of incest is its primordial form.

The child who is loved by both his parents and not harshly subjugated by taboo will trustfully experience his erotic desire towards his mother without being aggressive towards his father. The natural filial rivalry is moderated by love. Oedipus fucked Jocasta, his mother, and killed Laius, his father, it is true. But both had previously wanted to kill him. The son, in spite of his love competition for his mother, never attacks a kind father. It is only the incestuous prohibition, harshly imposed upon him by his father, that stirs up the desire for revenge. It is not love towards his mother but hatred towards his father that leads to this tragedy.

The results are quite different when parents use obscene language and put names to incest. In this way they are authorizing desire. It is the only means of genuinely overcoming the taboo. Furthermore, it is the only benevolent attitude towards the son, since the small child who is able to talk about his incestuous desires stops being a slave to them. This is the invaluable benefit from making conscious the unconscious.

Conscious thought allows for a higher form of control over the impulses. This is the basis of psychoanalytical therapy. When we speak of instincts, according to Freud, we do not make them vanish, this would be "impossible and besides it would not be desirable." What we achieve instead is "a submission of the instinct."[19] That is to say, only by talking about sexuality are we able to control it. Psychoanalysis, by employing obscene language, thus fulfills the moral ideal of the Greek philosopher, Aristyppus de Cirene (360 B.C.), who maintained (Diog. L. II. 75) that

> I possess but I am not possessed, since dominating pleasures and not being dominated by them is excellent, and not abstaining from them.[20]

IV

Freud splendidly revealed to the world his skill at interpretation during his famous analysis of a phobia in a five-year-old child. This is known as the case of Hans. Reported in 1908, this was the first psychoanalysis of a child, and curiously, it was conducted almost entirely through the mail! The father, an admirer of Freud, carried out the treatment under the epistolary guidance of the creator of psychoanalysis.

Hans was terrified of horses. His phobia for a while

even prevented him from going outside, and he lived a severely limited kind of life. The symptom was in fact a displacement: the horse represented his father. As he intensely desired his mother, he was unconsciously frightened of his father.

Freud met the boy only once. During that interview his participation was deep and bright:

> Then I started explaining to him that he was frightened of his father precisely because he loved his mother so much. He believed, no doubt, that his father did not take well that love and this was not true; his father also loved him much and he could confess without fear all his things to him. Long before he was born I knew a little Hans was going to be born who would deeply love his mother, and that he would be frightened of his father and I told all this to his father.[21]

Freud did not tell Hans he should renounce his desires. On the contrary, he stated that his father knew about them and accepted them! He did not condemn instinct but demolished moral conscience.[22] The first would have been an admonition that left the taboo intact; the second constituted an authentic liberation from it. From that consultation onwards, the psychic state of the child evolved until he was completely cured.

D. H. Lawrence, one of the most remarkable figures in contemporary English literature, accused Freud of fostering the violation of the taboo of incest.[23] The charge was unfortunate and, no doubt, gratuitous. The psychoanalytic patient does not consummate incest (as Hans did not), but what happens instead is that he talks about it. He does so *sans peur et sans reproche* (without fear and without reproach). He thinks of incest and does so to the ultimate, that is, obscenely. In this way, as Freud pointed out, when man overcomes "the horror of the idea of incest with his mother or sister"[24]—and the woman with her father or brother—they are able to recover their healthy, lustful approach to life.

V
FREEDOM

"I am still a liberal of the old mark."

SIGMUND FREUD
(Letter to Arnold Zweig, November 26, 1930)

Jurists are fond of teaching that criminal law has evolved considerably since the era of taboos, passing through the period of collective revenge, such as the *faida* of the ancient Germans, and the law of the Talion, "eye for eye, tooth for tooth"; through the period of compensation for offenses by means of a system of payment; and so on, until finally coming to the rational form of civilized legal codes.[25] So for them, taboos do not play a role in judicial life anymore, and its study therefore is relegated to the study of legal history.

This interpretation of the development of criminal law is optimistic, and after our study it is, besides, unsustainable. The legal condemnation of "dirty" words constitutes a refutation of such an interpretation. The taboo still placidly survives in the penal code! Evidently, primitive thought is so rooted in us that "our resemblances with the savage are still much more numerous than our differences."[26] Freud knew that very well:

> Of all the erroneous and superstitious beliefs of Mankind thought to have been overcome, there is none whose

> remnants are not currently found among us, in the lowest levels of civilized people or in the higher classes of the cultured society. What has become alive once firmly clings to keep its existence.[27]

And yet, for the preservation of a healthy society, "dirty" words must have a legitimate place in our daily life. Obscene words should be included in dictionaries–along with all other words. Moreover, they should enjoy the full freedom of spoken and written language at schools and colleges, as well as in the newspapers, and on radio and television. By setting the language free we are also releasing the soul. Only then will man be able to escape from the cruel and archaic psychic coercion of taboo, recover his moral independence, and widen his intelligence.

Condemnation of dirty words is a relic of our ancestral past that carries with it the imprint of the terrible prohibitions that gave rise to it. It is an anachronistic piece in our civilized world. Therefore, it is necessary to overcome this moral inertia. Obscene language should no longer be persecuted, atavistically, by law; on the contrary, it should be subjected to its tutorship.

The human being has the right to obscenity because he has the right to think, feel, and openly express his erotic emotions; because he has the right to enjoy passion; because he has the right to his mental and physical integrity, by faithfully evoking his incestuous fantasies and memories; because he has the right to develop his intelligence without censorship.

The findings of psychoanalysis leave no doubt about the legitimacy of this requirement. In obscene language the very essence of our being is revealed, the *ipsa hominis essentia.* With it the mysterious and eternal instincts are expressed in their most pure and transparent form, without veils and modesty. Passions are revealed, and man is able to discover himself as never before, understanding in full the voluptuous message from his entrails, and thereby achieving a rapturous certainty of who he was, is, and will be.

Notes

CHAPTER 1

1. S. Freud, Totem and taboo, in *The Standard Edition of the Complete Psychological Works of Sigmund Freud,* ed. J. Strachey (London: Hogarth Press and the Institute of Psychoanalysis, 1953–1974), vol. 13.
2. J. G. Frazer, *The Golden Bough: A Study in Magic and Religion* (New York: St. Martins, 1954), vol. 12.
3. Voltaire, *Love Letters to His Niece,* ed. and trans. T. Besterman (London: William Kimber & Co., 1958).

CHAPTER 2

1. H. H. Montgomery, *History of Pornography* (Buenos Aires: La Pleyade, 1973), vol. 1, p. 8.

2. W. Shakespeare, *As You Like It,* ed. J. Bisson (New York: Oxford University Press, 1941), 2.7.
3. H. H. Montgomery, vol. 1, p. 7.
4. S. Freud, Freud's psychoanalytic procedure, in *Standard Edition,* vol. 7.
5. S. Freud, Fragment of an analysis of a case of hysteria, in *Standard Edition,* vol. 7.
6. Ibid.
7. S. Freud, *Psychoanalysis and Faith: Dialogues with the Reverend Oskar Pfister,* ed. E. F. Freud and H. Meng, trans. E. Mosbacher (London: Hogarth Press, 1963).
8. E. Jones, *Life and Work of Sigmund Freud* (New York: Basic Books, 1953–1957), vol. 1.
9. Ibid.
10. *History of Psychoanalysis* (Buenos Aires: Paidos, 1968), vol. 4, p. 123.
11. L. de Marchi, *Sex and Civilization* (Buenos Aires: Helios, 1961), vol. 2, p. 69.
12. S. Freud, Letter on standing as regards Judaism.
13. W. Durant, *Our Oriental Heritage,* vol. 1 of *Story of Civilization* (New York: Simon & Schuster, 1935).
14. S. Freud, *A Psychoanalytic Dialogue: The Letters of Sigmund Freud and Karl Abraham, 1907–1926* (New York: Basic Books, 1965).
15. E. Jones, *Sigmund Freud,* vol. 1.
16. S. Freud, Sandor Ferenczi (Obituary), in *Standard Edition,* vol. 22.
17. S. Ferenczi, *On Obscene Words.*
18. Ibid.
19. H. Miller, *Tropic of Capricorn* (New York: Grove, 1962).
20. Plato, *Republic,* 2d ed., rev., 2 vols., ed. J. Adam (New York: Cambridge University Press, n.d.).
21. A. Garma, Sadism and masochism in human conduct, *Journal of Clinical Psychopathology* 6(1944–1945):1.

CHAPTER 3

1. *Song of Solomon* 4:5.
2. *Song of Solomon* 8:6–8.
3. J. Pijoan, *History of Art* (Barcelona: Salvat, 1970), vol. 6, p. 189.

4. L. de Marchi, vol. 2, p. 48.
5. Ibid., p. 42.
6. J. Corominas, *Diccionario Crítico Etiomológico de la Lengua Española,* 6 vols. (New York: French & European Publications, 1976).
7. J. Pijoan, vol. 6, p. 102.
8. Ibid., p. 63.
9. Lo Duca, *History of Eroticism* (Buenos Aires: Sigla Veinte, 1970), vol. 2, p. 33.
10. J. G. Bourke, *Scatology and Civilization.*
11. H. Deutsch, *The Psychology of Women,* 2 vols. (New York: Grune & Stratton, 1944–1945).
12. P. Louÿs, *Songs of Bilitis* (Madrid: Bergua), 2.120.
13. J. Pijoan, vol. 6, p. 241.
14. Ibid., vol. 8, p. 113.
15. Ibid., p. 200.
16. P. Louÿs, *Aphrodite* (New York: AMS Press, 1896).
17. H. Deutsch.
18. Ibid.
19. C. J. Cela, vol. 2; and R. Spears, *Slang and Euphemism* (Middle Village, NY: Jonathan David, 1981).
20. S. Freud, Leonardo da Vinci and a memory of his childhood, in *Standard Edition,* vol. 11.
21. Ibid.
22. *Kama Sutra–Aranga Ranga: Vedas' Edition.*
23. *Eros in Greece* (Barcelona: Diamon, 1976), pp. 86, 97, 98.
24. *Eros to Pompeií* (Milan: Arnoldo Mondado, 1974), pp. 107, 165.
25. F. Doig-Kauffman, *Sexual Behavior in Ancient Peru* (Lima: Kompaktos, 1979), pp. 27, 49, 137, 139.
26. J. Pijoan, vol. 6, p. 117.
27. Ibid., p. 108.
28. Ibid., p. 25.
29. E.-C. Flamand, *The Renaissance* (Madrid: Aguilar, 1969), p. 201.
30. H. Miller.

CHAPTER 4

1. Goethe, *Faust,* trans. B. Taylor (New York: Crofts, 1946), part 2, act v, line 397.

2. S. Freud, The future prospects of psychoanalytic therapy, in *Standard Edition,* vol. 11.
3. S. Freud, Jokes and their relationship to the unconscious, in *Standard Edition,* vol. 7.
4. Ibid.
5. S. Freud, "Civilized" sexual morality and modern nervous illness, in *Standard Edition,* vol. 9.
6. S. Freud, Introductory lectures on psycho-analysis, in *Standard Edition,* vol. 15.
7. A. de Laiglesia, *Only Fools Die* (Barcelona: Planeta, 1955), pp. 100–101.
8. Ibid.
9. S. Freud, From the history of an infantile neurosis, in *Standard Edition,* vol. 17.
10. J. G. Bourke.
11. Ibid.
12. Marquis de Sade, *Philosophy in the Bedroom,* trans. R. Seaver and A. Wainhouse (New York: Grove, 1971).
13. Ibid.
14. J. G. Bourke.
15. Ibid.
16. Ibid.
17. Ibid.
18. Ibid.
19. Ibid.
20. Ibid.
21. Ibid.
22. Ibid.
23. Ibid.
24. Ibid.
25. Ibid.
26. Ibid., prologue.
27. A. Garma, *Sadism and Masochism.*
28. W. Durant and A. Durant, *Rousseau and Revolution,* vol. 10 of *Story of Civilization* (New York: Simon & Schuster, 1967).
29. Ibid.
30. Ibid.

31. Letter published in Camp de L'arpa Journal on Literature, no. 52.
32. J. G. Bourke.
33. Ibid.
34. C. J. Cela, vol. 2, p. 36.
35. S. Freud, Jokes, in *Standard Edition,* vol. 7.
36. G. Groddeck, *The Book of the Id: Psychoanalytic Letters to a Friend* (New York: Nervous and Mental Disease Publishing, 1928).
37. Ibid.
38. Voltaire, *Philosophic Dictionary,* trans. T. Besterman (New York: Penguin, 1984).
39. D. H. Lawrence, *Lady Chatterley's Lover* (New York: New American Library, 1959).

CHAPTER 5

1. Marquis de Sade.
2. D. H. Lawrence.
3. *Eros to Pompeii,* pp. 52, 152, 153, 154.
4. C. Darwin, *On the Origin of the Species* (Cambridge, MA: Harvard University Press, 1859).
5. Lo Duca, p. 49.
6. P. B. de Brantôme.
7. Dante Alighieri, *Inferno,* in *The Divine Comedy,* trans. J. B. Fletcher (New York: Columbia University Press, 1951), cantos 15–16.
8. L. de Marchi, p. 92.
9. P. B. de Brantôme.
10. S. Freud, Three essays on the theory of sexuality, in *Standard Edition,* vol. 7.
11. Ibid.
12. Marquis de Sade.
13. S. Ferenczi, *Thalassa: A Theory in Genitality* (New York: Psychoanalytic Quarterly, 1938).
14. Exodus 2:11.
15. H. Hentig, *Sorrow* (Madrid: Espasa Calpe, 1968), vol. 1, p. 418.
16. Ibid., vol. 1., p. 419.

17. L. de Marchi, vol. 2, p. 77.
18. H. Hentig, vol. 1., p. 425.
19. H. H. Montgomery, vol. 5, p. 148.
20. H. Hentig, vol. 1, p. 425.
21. H. H. Montgomery, vol. 5, p. 143.
22. Ibid., p. 154.
23. Ibid.
24. L. de Marchi, vol. 2, p. 78.
25. Ibid.
26. Ibid.
27. Ibid.
28. Ibid.
29. H. Hentig, vol. 2, p. 409.
30. Ibid.
31. Ibid.
32. Ibid.
33. Ibid., vol. 1, p. 420.
34. S. Freud, Interpretation of dreams, in *Standard Edition,* vol. 4.
35. H. Hentig, vol. 1, p. 418.
36. Ibid., vol. 2, p. 416.
37. Ibid.
38. S. Freud, The neuro-psychoses of defence, in *Standard Edition,* vol. 3.
39. H. Hentig, vol. 1, p. 418.
40. Ibid., p. 426.
41. E. Glover, *War, Sadism, and Pacifism: Three Essays* (London: Allen and Unwin, p. 1933).
42. W. Durant, *Our Oriental Heritage.*
43. H. Hentig, vol. 1, p. 316.
44. Ibid.
45. Ibid., p. 375.
46. Ibid., p. 431.
47. W. Durant, *The Renaissance,* vol. 5 of *Story of Civilization* (New York: Simon & Schuster, 1953).
48. J. Larteguy, *The Centurions* (Buenos Aires: Emece, 1975), p. 356.
49. C. Darwin.
50. R. Vavra, *Such Is the Real Nature of Horses* (New York: Morrow, 1979).

51. Ibid.
52. Ibid.
53. S. Freud, From the history of an infantile neurosis, in *Standard Edition,* vol. 17.
54. R. Vavra.
55. K. Lorenz, *On Aggression,* trans. M. K. Wilson (New York: Harcourt, Brace, Jovanovich, 1974).
56. C. E. Lujan, Journal of Universal Geography, p. 351.
57. Ibid., p. 350.
58. K. Lorenz.
59. R. Vavra.
60. K. Lorenz.
61. S. Freud, Totem and taboo, in *Standard Edition,* vol. 13.
62. T. Reik, *Ritual: Psycho-analytic Studies* (New York: Norton, 1931).
63. Ibid.
64. T. Reik, *Masochism in Modern Man,* trans. M. H. Biegal and G. M. Kurth (New York: Farrar & Rinehart, 1941).
65. S. Freud, Foreword to a book by Theodor Reik, vol. 3, p. 301.
66. W. Durant, *Life of Greece,* vol. 2 of *Story of Civilization* (New York: Simon & Schuster, 1939).
67. P. Calderón, *Life is a Dream,* trans. W. E. Colford (Hauppauge, NY: Barron, 1958), scene 19.
68. E. Jones, *Essays in Applied Psychoanalysis,* vol. 2, p. 195.
69. "Russian Religions," in *Encyclopaedia Britannica,* 14th ed. (New York: Encyclopaedia Britannica, 1929).
70. M. Tractenberg, *Circumcision* (Buenos Aires: Paidos, 1972), vol. 1, p. 31.
71. Ibid.
72. L. de Marchi, p. 65.
73. T. Reik, *Masochism in Modern Man.*
74. W. Durant, *The Age of Faith,* vol. 4 of *Story of Civilization* (New York: Simon & Schuster, 1950).
75. S. Freud, Some neurotic mechanisms in jealousy, paranoia and homosexuality, in *Standard Edition,* vol. 18.
76. W. Durant, *Caesar and Christ,* vol. 3 of *Story of Civilization* (New York: Simon & Schuster, 1944).

CHAPTER 6

1. Webster's Dictionary.
2. Voltaire, Philosophic Dictionary.
3. H. H. Montgomery, vol. 3, p. 104.
4. J. Pijoan, vol. 5, p. 241.
5. Ibid., p. 239.
6. G. Petronius, *The Satyricon,* 2d ed., rev., ed. E. T. Sage and B. G. Gilleland (New York: Irvington, 1969), pp. 138–142.
7. A. Garma, *The Psychoanalysis* (Buenos Aires: Paidos, 1978), p. 114.
8. B. Russell, *Marriage and Morals* (New York: Liveright, 1929).
9. S. Freud, *The Letters of Sigmund Freud and Karl Abraham.*
10. Ibid.
11. E. Jones, *Life and Work of Sigmund Freud.*
12. L. de Marchi, vol. 3, p. 137.
13. C. J. Cela, vol. 1, p. 57.
14. H. H. Montgomery, vol. 2., p. 53.
15. Ibid.
16. Ibid.
17. *Eros in Greece,* p. 82.
18. Aristophanes, *Lysistrata,* trans. D. Sutherland (New York: Harper & Row, 1961).
19. P. Louÿs, *Songs of Bilitis,* 3.224.
20. W. Durant and A. Durant, *The Age of Voltaire.*
21. Lo Duca, p. 58.
22. Ibid., p. 50.
23. S. Freud, Interpretation of dreams, in *Standard Edition,* vol. 4.
24. S. Bernfeld, S. Freud, 1882-1885, in *International Journal of Psycho-Analysis* 22(1951):204–217.
25. T. Reik, *Fragment of a Great Confession: A Psychoanalytic Autobiography* (New York: Farrar, Straus, 1949).
26. Ibid.
27. S. Freud, "Civilized" sexual morality, in *Standard Edition,* vol. 9.
28. F. Nietzsche, *Beyond Good and Evil* (Washington, DC: Regnery Gateway, 1955).
29. Aristotle, *Aristotle's Politics,* trans. H. G. Apostle and L. P. Gerson, Apostle Translations of Aristotle's Works Series, no. 7 (Grinnell, IA: Peripatetic Press, 1986).

30. Aristotle, *Aristotle's Metaphysics,* trans. H. G. Apostle, Apostle Translations of Aristotle's Works Series, no. 1 (Grinnell, IA: Peripatetic Press, 1979).
31. Ibid.
32. S. Freud, Psychoanalysis multiple concern, *Standard Edition,* vol. 2, p. 882.
33. S. Freud, Further remarks on the neuro-psychoses of defence, in *Standard Edition,* vol. 3.
34. S. Freud, Three essays on the theory of sexuality, in *Standard Edition,* vol. 7.

CHAPTER 7

1. S. Freud, Jokes, in *Standard Edition,* vol. 8.
2. S. Freud, Psychopathology of everyday life, in *Standard Edition,* vol. 6.
3. S. Freud, Jokes, in *Standard Edition,* vol. 8.
4. A. Schopenhauer, *Love, Women, and Death* (Buenos Aires: Malinca Pocket, 1964), p. 58.
5. Ovid, The art of love, in *The Art of Love and Other Poems,* Loeb Classical Library, no. 232 (Cambridge, MA: Harvard University Press, n.d.), vol. 2, pp. 679–680.
6. S. Freud, Medusa's head, in *Standard Edition,* vol. 18.
7. S. Freud, Interpretation of dreams, in *Standard Edition,* vol. 4.
8. S. Freud, Medusa's head, in *Standard Edition,* vol. 18.
9. *Mythology* (São Paulo: Victor Civita, 1973), vol. 2, p. 457.
10. J. Pijoan, vol. 6, p. 58.
11. S. Freud, Medusa's head, in *Standard Edition,* vol. 18.
12. F. Rabelais.
13. J. Corominas and R. Spears.
14. V. Nabokov, *Lolita* (New York: Putnam Publishing Group, 1972).
15. Ibid.
16. P. Neruda, *The Captain's Verses,* trans. D. D. Walsh (New York: New Directions, 1972).
17. P. Louÿs, *Aphrodite.*
18. M. J. Ferrater, *Philosophic Dictionary* (Buenos Aires: Sudamericana, 1965).

19. M. M. Garcia, *Kant's Philosophy* (Madrid: Espasa Calpe, 1975), vol. 6, p. 175.
20. A. Schopenhauer, *World as Will and Idea,* trans. R. B. Haldane and J. Kemp (New York: AMS Press, 1896, reprinted, n.d.), vol. 3.
21. C. Darwin.
22. A. France, *Thaïs* (New York: French & European Publications, 1960).
23. S. Freud, Three essays on the theory of sexuality, in *Standard Edition,* vol. 7.
24. W. Durant, *The Age of Faith.*
25. Dante Alighieri, *The New Life,* trans. T. Martin, Select Bibliographies Reprint Series (Salem, NH: Ayer Co. Pub., 1861, reprinted, n.d.), canto 3.
26. Ibid., canto 26.
27. Dante Alighieri, *Paradise,* in *The Divine Comedy,* canto 23, line 70.
28. Ibid., canto 30, line 28.
29. H. Miller.
30. P. B. de Brantôme.
31. D. H. Lawrence.
32. J. G. Frazer.

CHAPTER 8

1. Homer, *The Iliad,* trans. R. A. Lattimore (Chicago: University of Chicago Press, 1977), 14.222.
2. J. Corominas; R. Spears.
3. P. B. de Brantôme.
4. Ibid.
5. S. Ferenczi, Psychoanalysis of sexual habits, *International Journal of Psycho-Analysis* 6(1925):372–404; and *Further Contributions to the Theory and Technique of Psychoanalysis* (London: Hogarth Press and the Institute of Psychoanalysis, 1955).
6. S. Ferenczi, *Thalassa.*
7. C. J. Cela, vol. 1., p. 241.
8. S. Ferenczi, *Thalassa.*
9. O. Fenichel, *Psychoanalytic Theory of Neurosis* (New York: Norton, 1945).

10. Ovid, The art of love, lines 793–796.
11. F. Nietzsche, My sister and myself, in *Complete Works,* ed. O. Levy (New York: Macmillan, 1910–1914), vol. 12.
12. P. B. de Brantôme.
13. Ibid.
14. S. Freud, On the universal tendency to debasement in the sphere of love (Contributions to the psychology of love II), in *Standard Edition,* vol. 11.
15. O. Rank, *The Trauma of Birth* (New York: Harcourt Brace, 1929).
16. O. Rank, *The Myth of the Birth of the Hero,* trans. F. Robbins and S. E. Jollife (New York: Nervous and Mental Disease Publishing, 1914).
17. Ibid.
18. O. Rank, *The Trauma of Birth.*
19. S. Ferenczi, *Thalassa.*
20. L. de Marchi, vol. 1., p. 30.
21. Genesis 2:24.
22. Plato, *Symposium,* ed. K. G. Dover, Cambridge Greek and Latin Classic Series (New York: Cambridge University Press, 1980).
23. S. Ferenczi, Gulliver fantasies, *International Journal of Psycho-Analysis* 9(1928):283; and in *Final Contributions to the Problems and Methods of Psychoanalysis* (New York: Basic Books, 1955).
24. C. J. Cela, vol. 2., pp. 227, 324, 396, 397, 449.
25. Plato, *Symposium.*
26. A. Dumas, *La Dame aux Camélias,* trans. and ed. D. Coward, The World's Classics Series (New York: Oxford University Press, 1986).
27. S. Ferenczi, *Thalassa.*
28. S. Freud, Analysis terminable and interminable, in *Standard Edition,* vol. 23.
29. A. Schopenhauer, *The World as Will and Idea.*

CHAPTER 9

1. F. de Rojas, *Celestine,* trans. J. Mabbe (New York: Applause Theatre Book Publishers, 1986), 1.29.
2. W. Durant, *Our Oriental Heritage.*

3. Ibid.
4. W. Durant, *Life of Greece.*
5. Ibid.
6. W. Durant, *Caesar and Christ.*
7. Ibid.
8. Ibid.
9. W. Durant, *The Age of Faith.*
10. Ibid.
11. W. Durant, *The Renaissance.*
12. Ibid.
13. E. Jones, *Essays in Applied Psychoanalysis,* vol. II, p. 272.
14. O. Rank, *The Myth of the Hero's Birth.*
15. Ibid.
16. J. G. Frazer, vol. 24.
17. O. Rank, *The Myth of the Hero's Birth.*
18. D. F. Strauss, *New Life of Jesus* (Valencia, 1905), 2.57.40.
19. Diogenes Laertius, *Lives of Eminent Philosophers,* 2 vols. (Cambridge, MA: Harvard University Press, 1948), 3.1.2.
20. Plutarch, *Parallel Lives* (Cambridge, MA: Harvard University Press, n.d.), vol. 2.
21. Ovid, Fastos, in *The Art of Love and Other Poems,* 3.15.
22. D. Strauss, 2.57.40.
23. Suetonius, *Lives of the Caesars,* 2 vols., Loeb Classical Library (Cambridge, MA: Harvard University Press, n.d.).
24. Isaiah 7:14.
25. Matthew 1:18–25; Luke 1:26–38.
26. E. Jones, *Essays in Applied Psycho-analysis,* vol. 4, p. 334.
27. *Priapeos* (Madrid: Gredos, 1981), p. 45.
28. E. Jones, Ibid.
29. F. Rabelais.
30. S. Freud, Introductory lectures on psycho-analysis, in *Standard Edition,* vol. 15.
31. S. Freud, On the universal tendency to debasement in the sphere of love, in *Standard Edition,* vol. 11.
32. Virgil, *Eclogues,* ed. R. Coleman, Cambridge Greek and Latin Classic Series (New York: Cambridge University Press, 1977), 4.60-64.

CHAPTER 10

1. S. Freud, Freud's psychoanalytic procedure, in *Standard Edition,* vol. 7.
2. A. Garma, *Psychoanalysis,* vol. 14, p. 360.
3. R. Linton, *Study of Man: An Introduction* (New York: Appleton, 1936).
4. Ibid.
5. W. Durant, *Our Oriental Heritage.*
6. R. Linton, *Study of Man.*
7. W. Durant, *Our Oriental Heritage.*
8. R. Linton, *Study of Man.*
9. W. Durant, *Our Oriental Heritage.*
10. J. Pijoan, vol. 6, p. 276.
11. W. Durant, *The Age of Faith.*
12. Incest: The Last Taboo, *Reader's Digest,* September 1981.
13. M. Bonaparte, *Female Sexuality* (New York: International Universities Press, 1953).
14. E. Freeman, *Insights: Conversations with Theodor Reik* (Englewood Cliffs, NJ: Prentice-Hall, 1971).
15. J. Pijoan, vol. 8, p. 203.
16. O. Rank and H. Sachs, *The Significance of Psychoanalysis for the Mental Sciences* (New York: Nervous and Mental Disease Publishing, 1916).
17. S. Freud, Freud's psychoanalytic procedure, in *Standard Edition,* vol. 7.
18. A. Rascovsky, On filicide, *Bulletin of the Philadelphia Association for Psycho-Analysis,* abstracted by L. Wallance, 19(1969):248–252.
19. S. Freud, Analysis terminable and interminable, in *Standard Edition,* vol. 23.
20. R. Mondolfo, *The Ancient Thought* (Buenos Aires: Losado, 1964), vol. 1, p. 177.
21. S. Freud, Analysis of a phobia in a five-year-old boy, in *Standard Edition,* vol. 10.
22. S. Freud, Freud's psychoanalytic procedure, in *Standard Edition,* vol. 7.

23. P. Rieff, *Freud: The Mind of a Moralist,* rev. ed. (New York: Doubleday, 1961).
24. S. Freud, On the universal tendency to debasement in the sphere of love, in *Standard Edition,* vol. 11.
25. S. Soler, *Argentine Penal Law* (Buenos Aires: Tea, 1978), vol. 1, p. 39.
26. J. G. Frazer.
27. S. Freud, Analysis terminable and interminable, in *Standard Edition,* vol. 23.

References

Abraham, K. (1913). *Dreams and Myths: A Study in Race Psychology.* Trans. W. A. White. Nervous and Mental Disease Monograph Series, no. 15. New York: Journal of Nervous and Mental Disease Publishing.

Aristophanes (1961). *Lysistrata.* Trans. D. Sutherland. New York: Harper & Row.

Aristotle (1979). *Aristotle's Metaphysics.* Trans. H. G. Apostle. Apostle Translations of Aristotle's Works Series, no. 1. Grinnell, IA: Peripatetic Press.

_____ (1986). *Aristotle's Politics.* Trans. H. G. Apostle and L. P. Gerson. Apostle Translations of Aristotle's Works Series, no. 7. Grinnell, IA: Peripatetic Press.

Bergson, H. (1955). *Creative Mind: Introduction to Metaphysics.* 2d ed. Trans. M. L. Andison. New York: Philosophical Library.

Bernfeld, S. (1951). Sigmund Freud, M.D., 1882–1885. *International Journal of Psycho-Analysis* 22:204–217.

Bonaparte, M. (1953). *Female Sexuality.* New York: International Universities Press.

Bourke, J. G. (n.d.). *Scatology and Civilization.*

Brantôme, P. B. de (1933). *Lives of Fair & Gallant Ladies.* New York: Liveright.

Calderón, P. (1958). *Life is a Dream.* Trans. W. E. Colford. Hauppauge, NY: Barron.

Cela, C. J. (1978). *Secret Dictionary.* Madrid: Alianza.

Cervantes Saavedra, M. de (1880). *The History of Don Quixote of La Mancha.* Preceded by *A Short Notice of the Life and Works of Motteau* by H. Vannlaun. 4 vols. Ed. J. G. Lockhart. Darby, PA: Darby Books. Reprinted 1983.

Churchill, W. S. (1956–1958). *A History of the English Speaking Peoples.* 4 vols. New York: Dodd, Mead, & Co.

Corominas, J. (1976). *Diccionario Crítico Etimológico de la Lengua Espãñola.* 6 vols. New York: French & European Publications.

Dante Alighieri (1861). *The New Life.* Trans. T. Martin. Select Bibliographies Reprint Series. Salem, NH: Ayer Co. Pubs.

____ (1951). *The Divine Comedy.* Trans. J. B. Fletcher. New York: Columbia University Press.

Darwin, C. (1859). *On the Origin of the Species.* Cambridge, MA: Harvard University Press.

Deutsch, H. (1944–1945). *The Psychology of Women.* 2 vols. New York: Grune & Stratton.

Dictionary of the Spanish Language (1970). Royal Spanish Academy.

Donne, J. (1985). Everyman. In *The Complete English Poems of John Donne,* ed. C. A. Patrides. Totowa, NJ: Biblio Distribution Center, Division of Littlefield, Adams & Co.

Dumas, A. (1986). *La Dame aux Camélias.* Trans. and ed. D. Coward. The World's Classics Series. New York: Oxford University Press.

Durant, W. (1935). *Story of Civilization.* Vol. 1. *Our Oriental Heritage.* New York: Simon & Schuster.

____ (1939). *Story of Civilization.* Vol. 2. *Life of Greece.* New York: Simon & Schuster.

____ (1944). *Story of Civilization.* Vol. 3. *Caesar and Christ: A History of*

Roman Civilization from Its Beginning to A.D. 337. New York: Simon & Schuster.

____ (1950). *Story of Civilization.* Vol. 4. *The Age of Faith.* New York: Simon & Schuster.

____ (1953). *Story of Civilization.* Vol. 5. *The Renaissance.* New York: Simon & Schuster.

Durant, W., and Durant, A. (1965). *Story of Civilization.* Vol. 9. *The Age of Voltaire.* New York: Simon & Schuster.

____ (1967). *Story of Civilization.* Vol. 10. *Rousseau and Revolution.* New York: Simon & Schuster.

Espasa Calpe Encyclopaedia (1926). Bilbao.

Encyclopaedia Brittanica (1929). 14th ed. 14 vols. New York: Encyclopaedia Britannica.

Eros to Pompeii (1974). Milan: Arnoldo Mondadori.

Eros in Greece (1976). Barcelona: Daimon.

Fenichel, O. (1945). *Psychoanalytic Theory of Neurosis.* New York: Norton.

Ferenczi, S. (1925). Psychoanalysis of sexual habits. *International Journal of Psycho-Analysis* 6:372–404. And in *Further Contributions to the Theory and Technique of Psychoanalysis.* London: Hogarth Press and the Institute of Psychoanalysis, 1926.

____ (1928). Gulliver fantasies. *International Journal of Psychoanalysis* 9:283. And in *Final Contributions to the Problems and Methods of Psychoanalysis,* pp. 41–60. New York: Basic Books, 1955.

____ (1938). *Thalassa: A Theory in Genitality.* New York: Psychoanalytic Quarterly.

____ (1952). *First Contributions to Psychoanalysis.* London: Hogarth Press.

Ferrater, M. J. (1965). *Philosophic Dictionary.* Buenos Aires: Sudamericana.

Flamand, E.-C. (1969). *The Renaissance.* Madrid: Aguilar.

France, A. (1960). *Thaïs.* New York: French & European Publications.

Frazer, J. G. (1954). *The Golden Bough: A Study in Magic and Religion.* 13 vols. New York: St. Martins.

Freeman, E. (1971). *Insights: Conversations with Theodor Reik.* Englewood Cliffs, NJ: Prentice-Hall.

Freud, S. (1953–1974). *The Standard Edition of the Complete Psychological*

Works of Sigmund Freud. 24 vols. Ed. J. Strachey. London: The Hogarth Press and the Institute of Psychoanalysis.

——— (1948). *Sigmund Freud: Obras Completas.* 2 vols. Madrid: Editorial Biblioteca Nueva.

——— (1963). *Psychoanalysis and Faith: Dialogues with the Reverend Oskar Pfister.* Ed. E. L. Freud and H. Meng. Trans. E. Mosbacher. London: Hogarth Press.

——— (1965). *A Psychoanalytic Dialogue: The Letters of Sigmund Freud and Karl Abraham, 1907–1926.* New York: Basic Books.

Garcia, M. M. (1975). *Kant's Philosophy.* Madrid: Espasa Calpe.

Garma, A. (1944–1945). Sadism and masochism in human conduct. *Journal of Clinical Psychopathology* 6:1.

——— (1978). *The Psychoanalysis.* Buenos Aires: Paidos.

Glover, E. (1933). *War, Sadism, and Pacifism: Three Essays.* London: Allen and Unwin.

Goethe (1946). *Faust.* Trans. B. Taylor. New York: Crofts.

Groddeck, G. (1928). *The Book of the Id: Psychoanalytic Letters to a Friend.* New York: Nervous and Mental Disease Publishing.

Hentig, H. (1968). *Sorrow.* Madrid: Espasa Calpe.

History of Psychoanalysis (1968). Buenos Aires: Paidos.

Holy Bible (1980). Barcelona: Salvat.

Homer (1977). *The Iliad.* Trans. R. A. Lattimore. Chicago: University of Chicago Press.

Jones, E. (1953–1957). *Life and Work of Sigmund Freud.* 3 vols. New York: Basic Books.

——— (1964). *The Psychology of Religion.* London: Hogarth Press.

Kama Sutra–Aranga Ranga: Vedas' Edition. Ramos Mejia.

Kama Sutra of Vatsyayana (1981). Trans. S. C. Upadhyaya. New York: Apt. Books.

Kauffman-Doig, F. (1979). *Sexual Behavior in Ancient Peru.* Lima: Kompaktos.

Diogenes Laertius (1948). *Lives of Eminent Philosophers.* 2 vols. Cambridge, MA: Harvard University Press.

Laiglesia, A. de (1955). *Only Fools Die.* Barcelona: Planeta.

Larteguy, J. (1975). *The Centurions.* Buenos Aires: Emece.

Lawrence, D. H. (1959). *Lady Chatterley's Lover.* New York: New American Library.

Linton, R. (1936). *Study of Man: An Introduction.* New York: Appleton.

Lo Duca (1970). *History of Eroticism.* Buenos Aires: Siglo Veinte.

Lorenz, K. (1974). *On Aggression.* Trans. M. K. Wilson. New York: Harcourt, Brace Jovanovich.

Louÿs, P. (1896). *Aphrodite.* New York: AMS Press.

_____ (n.d.). *Songs of Bilitis.* Madrid: Bergua.

Lucretius (1950). *On the Nature of Things.* Trans. W. H. Brown. New Brunswick, NJ: Rutgers University Press.

Marchi, L. de (1961). *Sex and Civilization.* Buenos Aires: Helios.

Miller, H. (1962). *Tropic of Capricorn.* New York: Grove.

Mondolfo, R. (1964). *The Ancient Thought.* Buenos Aires: Losada.

Montgomery, H. H. (1973). *History of Pornography.* Buenos Aires: La Pleyade.

Mythology (1973). São Paulo: Victor Civita.

Nabokov, V. (1972). *Lolita.* New York: Putnam Publishing Group.

Neruda, P. (1972). *The Captain's Verses.* Trans. D. D. Walsh. New York: New Directions.

Nietzsche, F. (1910–1914). *Complete Works.* 18 vols. Ed. O. Levy. New York: Macmillan.

_____ (1955). *Beyond Good and Evil.* Washington, DC: Regnery Gateway.

Ovid (n.d.). *The Art of Love and Other Poems.* Loeb Classical Library, no. 232. Cambridge, MA: Harvard University Press.

Petronius, G. (1969). *The Satyricon.* 2d ed., rev. Eds. E. T. Sage and B. G. Gilleland. New York: Irvington.

Pijoan, J. (1970). *History of Art.* Barcelona: Salvat.

Plato (1980). *Symposium.* Cambridge Greek and Latin Classic Series. Ed. K. J. Dover. New York: Cambridge University Press.

_____ (n.d.). *Republic.* 2d ed., rev. 2 vols. Ed. J. Adam. New York: Cambridge University Press.

Plutarch, (n.d.). *Parallel Lives.* 11 vols. Cambridge, MA: Harvard University Press.

Priapeos (1981). Madrid: Gredos.

Quevedo y Villegas, F. G. de (1926). *Choice Humorous Satirical Works.* Ed. C. Duff. Trans. R. L'Estrange and J. Stevens. Library of World Literature Series. Westport, CT: Hyperion Press. Reprinted 1976.

Rabelais, F. (1929). *Gargantua and Pantagruel.* 2 vols. Totowa, NJ: Biblio Distribution Center, Division of Littlefield, Adams, and

Co. Reprinted 1980.
Rank, O. (1914). *The Myth of the Birth of the Hero: A Psychological Interpretation by Mythology.* Trans. F. Robbins and S. E. Jollife. New York: Nervous and Mental Disease Publishing.
——— (1929). *The Trauma of Birth.* New York: Harcourt Brace.
Rank, O., and Sachs, H. (1916). *The Significance of Psychoanalysis for the Mental Sciences.* New York: Nervous and Mental Disease Publishing.
Rascovsky, A. (1969). On filicide. Presented at Los Angeles Psychoanalytic Society, Los Angeles, CA, January 1969. And in *Bulletin of the Philadelphia Association for Psychoanalysis* 19: 248–252, 1969.
Reik, T. (1931). *Ritual: Psycho-analytic Studies.* New York: Norton.
——— (1941). *Masochism in Modern Man.* Trans. M. H. Biegal and G. M. Kurth. New York: Farrar & Rinehart.
——— (1945). *Psychology of Sex Relations.* New York: Farrar & Rinehart.
——— (1948, 1949). *Listening with the Third Ear: The Inner Experience of a Psychoanalyst.* New York: Farrar, Straus.
——— (1949). *Fragment of a Great Confession: A Psychoanalytic Autobiography.* New York: Farrar, Straus.
Rieff, P. (1961). *Freud: The Mind of the Moralist.* Rev. ed. New York: Doubleday.
Rojas, F. de (1986). *Celestina.* Trans. J. Mabbe. New York: Applause Theatre Book Publishers.
Russell, B. (1929). *Marriage and Morals.* New York: Liveright.
Sade, Marquis de (1971). *Philosophy in the Bedroom.* Trans. R. Seaver and A. Wainhouse. New York: Grove.
Schopenhauer, A. (1964). *Love, Women, and Death.* Buenos Aires: Malinca Pocket.
——— (1896). *World as Will and Idea.* 3 vols. Trans. R. B. Haldane and J. Kemp. New York: AMS Press.
Shakespeare, W. (1941). *As You Like It.* Ed. J. Bisson. New York: Oxford University Press.
Soler, S. (1978). *Argentine Penal Law.* Buenos Aires: Tea.
Spears, R. A. (1981). *Slang and Euphemism: A Dictionary of Oaths, Curses, Insults, Sexual Slang and Metaphor, Racial Slurs, Drug Talk, Homosexual Lingo, and Related Matters.* Middle Village, NY:

Jonathan David.
Strauss, D. F. (1905). *New Life of Jesus.* Valencia.
Suetonius (n.d.). *Lives of the Caesars.* 2 vols. Loeb Classical Library. Cambridge, MA: Harvard University Press.
Tractenberg, M. (1972). *Circumcision.* Buenos Aires: Paidos.
Vavra, R. (1979). *Such Is the Real Nature of Horses.* New York: Morrow.
Virgil (1977). *Eclogues.* Ed. R. Coleman. Cambridge Greek and Latin Classic Series. New York: Cambridge University Press.
Voltaire (1958). *Love Letters to His Niece.* Ed. and trans. T. Besterman. London: William Kimber & Co.
____ (1984). *Philosophical Dictionary.* Trans. T. Besterman. New York: Penguin.

Index